JIT Factory Revolution

A PICTORIAL GUIDE TO FACTORY DESIGN OF THE FUTURE

Hiroyuki Hirano, Editor-in-Chief
JIT Management Laboratory Company Ltd. (Tokyo)

Dr. JT. Black, Editor, English Edition

Productivity Press
Cambridge, Massachusetts
Norwalk, Connecticut

Productivity Press
P.O. Box 3007
Cambridge, Massachusetts 02140
U.S.A.

telephone: (617) 497-5146
telefax: (617) 868-3524

Library of Congress Catalog Card Number: 88-29007
ISBN: 0-915299-44-5

Cover and book design by Joyce C. Weston
Typeset by Rudra Press, Cambridge, Massachusetts
Printed and bound by Arcata/Halliday
Printed in the United States of America

Library of Congress Cataloging-in-Publication Data

Hirano, Hiroyuki.
 JIT factory revolution.

 Includes index
  1. Just-in-time systems.   2. Factory management.
 I. JIT Management Laboratory Company.   II. Title.
 TS155.H49   1989   658.5   88-29007
 ISBN 0-915299-44-5

92 10 9 8 7 6 5 4

Contents

Publisher's Preface by Norman Bodek   v
Foreword by Dr. JT. Black, Auburn University   vi
Introduction by Hiroyuki Hirano, JIT Management Laboratory
  Company   ix
Introduction to the English Edition   x

JIT Factory Revolution   1
     Yen Appreciation: Ordeal for Survival   2

1. Introduction to Just-In-Time (JIT)   4
     Can Traditional Methods Save You?   4
     You've Seen this Situation, Haven't You?   6
     JIT Structure   13
     Introduction Procedure   14
     Improvement at a Glance   16

2. Awareness Revolution   18
     Ten Principles for Improvement   18
     Just-In-Time   20
     Motion and Work   23
     Surface Improvement vs. Real Improvement   24
     Procedure for Improving Productivity and Eliminating Waste   27

3. The 5s's   28
     Running a Red Tag Campaign   32
     Keeping Shelves in Order   36
     Keeping Storage Areas in Order   45
     Keeping the Workplace in Order   46
     Keeping Worktables in Order   53
     Keeping the Office in Order   56

4. Flow Manufacturing   64
     Lot Production vs. Flow Manufacturing   66
     Cellular Shop   68
     U-Shaped Line   70
     Cellular Manufacturing and Assembly   74
     Multi-Process Handling   76
     Cycle Time   78
     Standing (Chair-Free) Operations   80
     Mutual Line Assistance   89
     Small In-Line Machines   92

5. **Standard Operations** **102**
      Operations Charts 104

6. **Multi-Process Handling** **110**
      Multi-Machine Handling and Multi-Process Handling 112
      Casters 119

7. **Reducing Worker Hours** **122**
      Reduction in Labor vs. Reduction in Workers 124
      A Cell 126

8. **Leveling Production** **128**
      How to Make a Production Plan 130

9. *Jidoka* **(Automation with a Human Touch)** **134**
      Evolution toward Autonomation (*Jidoka*) 137
      Machine Independence 138
      A Zero-Defect Operation 141

10. **Changeover** **144**
      Changeover Procedures 146

11. **Quality Assurance** **158**
      Starting and Maintaining a Companywide Defect Prevention
         (*Poka-yoke)* Program 160

12. *Kanban* **166**
      Using *Kanban* as a Work Order 168

13. **Visual Control** **174**
      Andon (Line-Stop Alarm Light) 177
      Signboards 178

14. **Maintenance and Safety** **198**
      Maintenance 200
      Safety 203

About the Editors **204**
Index **206**

Publisher's Preface

We are honored to publish *JIT Factory Revolution,* the first pictorial book on just-in-time manufacturing. It is current information urgently needed by all those studying and applying manufacturing methods today.

Just-in-time represents a whole new process of continuous improvement within an organization. It is not just a one-shot process to reduce inventory. It is a continual process of change focused on delivering quality products at the exact time and in the exact quantities needed.

Quality under the just-in-time umbrella refers to quality goods as well as to quality service and quality of work life for everyone involved. In just-in-time's focus on the total elimination of waste, waste is anything that does not add value.

For making this book available to Productivity Press, I thank Mr. Hajime Kitamura, director of the publications division of the Nikkan Kogyo Shimbun Company Ltd. of Tokyo. The NKS people told us the book was valuable — and once we had it in English, we agreed. The English translation was the project of Ms. Reiko Kano, our company's interpreter, with assistance from Michael Kelsey of Inari Translations.

In content, the book is as good as it is due to the direct intervention of special editor Dr. JT. Black, Director of Auburn University's Advanced Manufacturing Technology Center and Professor of Industrial Engineering. Dr. Black made us aware that this book was more than a picture book — that it was one of the first books to talk about manufacturing cells and their design. He edited and focused the translation and, in the Foreword, tells exactly how he perceives the book's applicability.

Special thanks to managing editor Cheryl Berling Rosen, production manager Esmé McTighe, and production coordinator David Lennon for hard work and dedication to this project. My gratitude goes to Joyce C. Weston, Boston-based artist, for designing the text and photo layout of the book and its jacket. Rudra Press's Caroline Kutil, Michele Seery, Jane Donovan and Susan Cobb skillfully handled the typesetting, layout and design, and paste-up of this challenging and exciting project.

Lastly, I thank the original Japanese editor, Mr. Hiroyuki Hirano, of the JIT Management Laboratory Company in Japan. He initiated this book project in 1987 as a manual to help create in Japanese workers a JIT state of mind. We gratefully acknowledge his efforts.

Norman Bodek
President and CEO
Productivity, Inc.

Foreword

My thanks go to Norman Bodek and Cheryl Rosen for giving me the opportunity to contribute to *JIT Factory Revolution: A Pictorial Guide to Factory Design of the Future*.

Most of what is presented in this book has not been described in any detail in other JIT books and the reason is quite obvious. This book concentrates on the *design of the manufacturing system*. Other JIT books have concentrated on the operational and managerial aspects of JIT. Why is JIT a revolution? Because it requires a systems-level conversion of the manufacturing system. When the manufacturing system is changed, all other parts of the company (the production system) are also changed.

Specifically, this book graphically presents aspects of plant design and JIT manufacturing. Many examples of manufacturing cells are given. The task of designing manufacturing cells is every bit as complex as the design of the company's products and, certainly, every bit as important when it comes to quality and cost.

I have believed for many years that the secret to success of the Toyota Motor Company was in the redesign of their manufacturing system. I never believed that their process technology was any better or their work force superior to that of the United States. But, clearly, their manufacturing system differed from ours. It was not a job shop, functionally arranged. It was a system of linked manufacturing and assembly cells. The cells were U-shaped and matched the final assembly lines in production rates.

The man who invented this system, Taiichi Ohno, never gave it a name other than the Toyota Production System, referring to the entire plant. I think the U-shaped design should be called a *cell*. While often missed by many authors and sellers of JIT, manufacturing cells are the basic building blocks of JIT manufacturing systems.

A manufacturing system is a collection of manufacturing processes and other elements (such as tooling, workholders, material-handling devices) plus people arranged to produce products. The system is characterized by measurable parameters such as throughput time, production rates, percent defects, work-in-progress, and so forth. The inputs to the system are materials, information, energy, and social and political pressures.

The manufacturing system is the heart of the production system which includes all the other elements, from research and development to customer sales. Because the traditional or classical manufacturing system was functionally designed, so also was the production system. Think about the production system in your company. Are all the people grouped functionally? Are all the design engineers in a room separate from the accountants who are separate from the production planning and control people? If your system is functionally designed, a job shop, you will have a difficult time integrating your factory with modern technology.

This book describes a new manufacturing system design — cells. The chief design criteria for a cell is that it is flexible. "Oh," you say, "No problem! I know what a flexible manufacturing system is. In fact, we have an FMS in our plant." Sorry, cells differ from FMSs in many ways. Cells can have several types of flexibility. A cell can adapt to changes in the product demand quite easily. That is, the production rate for the cell can be readily changed, simply by adding or subtracting (parts of) workers. You have already observed this idea if you have gone to Wendy's, a fast-food manufacturing cell for hamburgers. At lunchtime, many workers are in the cell, so the production rate is high. In midafternoon, when business is slow, only a few workers are in the cell. This is one type of flexibility you will find described in this book. You will see many examples of unseated (walking) workers. Like the workers at Wendy's, the people in a cell are unseated, multifunctional workers, capable of performing many tasks and duties in addition to running different processes.

With another type of flexibility, the cell can adapt to changes in the product mix. Each cell makes a family of parts. Let's say the family has four different parts. All four parts have the same sequence of processes. When the parts are different in size, their machining times differ because the machining time depends upon the length of the cut. However, altering the machining time will not disturb the cell's production rate because the cell cycle time is dictated by the time it takes the worker to walk around the cell. Thus, the mix of parts in the family can be changed without disturbing the production rate.

With a third type of flexibility, the cell can adapt to changes in the product design. Redesign of the cell is often required. Thus, the equipment must be relocated on the plant floor. You will note that many of the machines shown in this book are on wheels, making the job of restructuring the cell much easier. Twenty years ago, the job of redesigning the manufacturing system was called "plant layout." It was done by the industrial engineers when a new plant was being built or it simply developed as the plant grew. Once the plant was laid out, the job was considered to be done. Now we recognize that to be flexible, the manufacturing system must be constantly redesigned to improve quality, reduce costs, decrease throughput time, and lower in-process inventory.

Notice that *within the cells*, parts move one at a time from machine to machine. This one-piece part movement eliminates queues (storage banks) between the processes, reduces material handling, and saves floor space. In order to manufacture with cells, setup time must be reduced, so the rapid exchange of tooling and dies is very important. The machines must also be improved to inform operators when something is going wrong. The operators can solve the problem quickly. Therefore, measures to prevent defects and machine breakdowns must be implemented. Some of these techniques are shown in this book.

Between the cells, parts are moved by small lots of uniform size. The number of lots is minimized. The number and movement of lots are controlled by *kanban*. Material is being pulled as needed by the downstream processes. The critical functions of production and inventory control are infused within the manufacturing system. Thus, *kanban* links the cells to the subassembly and final assembly lines. Many authors have described *kanban* but, for it to work, the manufacturing system must be redesigned.

I hope you will enjoy this pictorial plant tour as much as I did. Don't take this book lightly just because it is filled with pictures. Much can be learned about manufacturing systems design from it. If a picture is worth a thousand words, then this book is an encyclopedia of information about JIT manufacturing.

Dr. JT. Black
Auburn University

Introduction

Japan's strong industrial reputation is well-known around the world. Although the names "Toyota" and "Matsushita" come to mind, the real strength behind Japanese industry is its mid- to small-size enterprises called *shitauke,* or subcontractors. Of the 100 to 200 mid- to small-size companies that submitted their photographs to this *JIT Factory Revolution* project, 90 percent are subcontractors. I hope these photographs will impart a sense of the all-out effort these companies have been making to survive.

The conventional description of just-in-time (JIT) is a system for manufacturing and supplying goods that are needed, when they are needed, and in the exact quantities needed. This, however, only defines JIT intellectually. The people in the workplace, using their minds, gaining experience, and sweating their way to improvement, don't define JIT this way. For them, JIT means trimming losses. When JIT is internalized, the waste around a factory is systematically trimmed away. To do this, traditional and fixed ideas are useless.

JIT trims losses. *JIT Factory Revolution,* I hope, will go beyond an academic understanding to give the reader a visceral experience. Toward this end, it is impossible to separate JIT from the actual workplace. Japan has progressed industrially because of its steadfast hold on the workplace. The workplace runs the gamut of emotions — from tension and excitement, to disappointment and joy. In short, it is the seat of our existence.

In a JIT environment, the workplace is the best instructor because it reflects life. In a real workplace, we observe real things and learn to improve real situations. These "3 reals" are essential to fundamental just-in-time. I can state confidently that a country that forgets these things will see its industry rapidly disappear.

We gratefully acknowledge the companies photographed in this book. All members of the JIT Management Laboratory Company Ltd., they include:

Kōyō Denshi
Union Denki
Sunwave Kogyo
Kashiyama Press Kogyo
Nihon Mokuzai Kogyo
Akita Shindengen
Polar Kasei Kogyo
Tateshina Seisakusho

Fukuda ME Kōgyo
Miyamoto Seisakusho
Miyuki Seiki
Yamazawa Denki
Ninomiya Denki
Nihon Barufu
Takahata Denshi
Fuji Kogyo

Hiroyuki Hirano

March 1989
JIT Management Laboratory

Introduction to the English Edition

A number of years ago, when a certain factory was receiving guidance in JIT, a top-level manager suddenly made the following remark: "Our factory is improving and changing significantly. Those of us here now can see that. But how can we pass on to our future employees the sense that this factory revolution is necessary for our survival? Could we take photographs for the record, scenes of the actual work areas, as evidence of this battle?"

This is how the idea was announced to various JIT-guided companies, and the collection of photographic records called *JIT Factory Revolution* was born. It was called an historical record because our aim was to express the living appearance of the manufacturing workplace just as it was. We wanted no cosmetic gloss or embellishment. The intent was to portray the dramatic battle for life in the workplace. The word "battle" necessarily implies an enemy. This enemy is not the United States nor Europe; not the newly industrialized countries (NICs) nor rivals within Japan. The enemy is ourselves.

We must stop doing things the way we always have; throw out our personal predispositions and begin with a fresh mind. This is not simply a matter of improvement but revolution for the sake of the factory's survival. The face of Japanese industry is composed of large enterprises such as Toyota and Matsushita. Its structural foundation, however, is the group of mid- to small-size subcontractors to whom this book is dedicated.

Hiroyuki Hirano

March 1989
JIT Management Laboratory

JIT Factory Revolution

Yen Appreciation: Ordeal for Survival

- We often hear the words "slow economy."
- For many people in today's society, basic needs have been satisfied. Most of us have access to clothing, food, a place to live, television, and an automobile. But even in these good times, we can't expect Japan's domestic market to continue growing.
- Our Japanese dependence on exports makes us sometimes wonder if we, in fact, export too much.

- One problem is the appreciation of the yen, which never seems to stop. Japanese export-oriented companies are struggling hard to survive.
- With friction growing between Japan and its trading partners, newly industrializing countries (NICs) are taking the opportunity to catch up with Japan.
- Japan's major export products, electrical appliances such as televisions and videocassette recorders (VCRs) and even automobiles, are caught in the crisis.
- Japanese manufacturing companies no longer can afford to be dependent on others. To show immediate profits, they must start a *JIT factory revolution*.

1. Introduction to Just-In-Time (JIT)

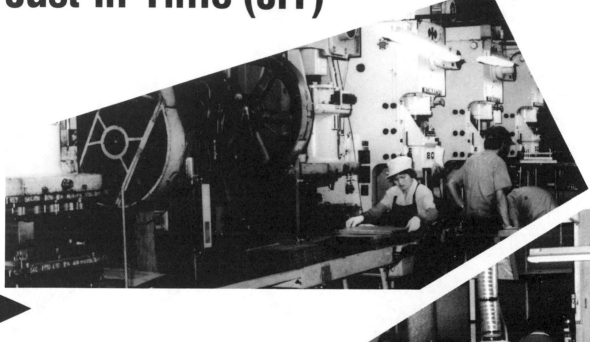

Can Traditional Methods Save You?

Inventory

- "If inventory conditions continue this way, we'll be out of business." Does your president shudder when going over inventory figures?
- Inventory hides other serious problems such as parts shortages, equipment breakdowns, and uneven production levels. First, eliminate the monster (Inventory!) and then solve these problems.

Defects!

- "Defects never decrease!" "I'm tired of customer returns." Does your plant manager complain like this?
- Producing a single defect can destroy your credibility. We must create defect-free processes.

Large lot production

- Are the words "economic lot" still prevailing in your factory? If so, remember that this concept is dead.
- We must move toward producing more diversified products.

Why not produce goods that are needed in the
needed quantities at the needed times?

Rising costs

- "It's impossible to reduce costs further." Does your section manager think
  like this?
- Improvement begins with believing that costs can always be reduced.

Delivery delays

- "Hey, another rush order!" "We already have enough rush orders." Do your line
  workers make these remarks?
- Meeting delivery times is basic for survival and requires a more flexible
  manufacturing system.

You've Seen this Situation, Haven't You?

We often come across situations like those in these two factory photographs. Workers appear to be working hard. If this was your company, knowing the efforts being made to increase efficiency, you would probably say nothing can be done about it because further improvement requires a more stable sales-based production schedule. This infers, however, that the customer is at fault. By observing other companies in the same industry, you will discover how some do well and maintain their profitability.

Temporary storage of wire harnesses: Is it really temporary? When will these quasi products be moved?

Storage for wire harness defectives: Profits are impossible with so many defectives.

You've Seen this Situation, Haven't You?

Things are piled directly on the floor.
Boxes stack up. It's impossible to find
anything.

What are the fan and cardboard boxes doing there?

Do the *kanban* that say "quasi product" tell the truth?

The shelves are better than the floor but are still disorganized.

Parts are piled up. When do you use shelves? What is where and where is what?

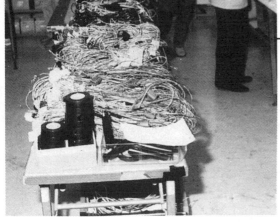

Harness assembly line: Can you pick up the harness in the middle of the pile without causing others to fall to the floor?

Electronic parts assembly line: It's common practice for the operators to sit.

Materials storage: When will these materials get used?

Workers sitting along the conveyor.

Electronic parts materials storage: A sign on the shelf says "OK to Ship." Does this mean it is the shelf for finished products?

You've Seen this Situation, Haven't You?

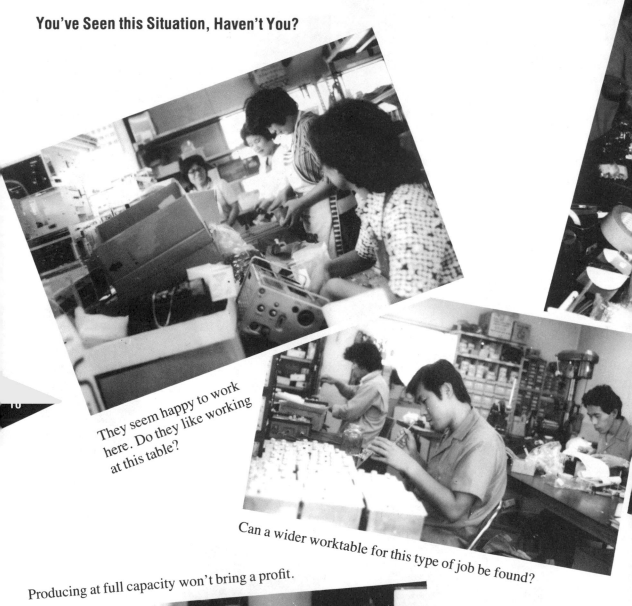

They seem happy to work here. Do they like working at this table?

Can a wider worktable for this type of job be found?

Producing at full capacity won't bring a profit.

只今出庫中
QR 1100
501AX

The sign says "OK to Ship Now."
How can we tell what's being
shipped?

The table is covered with work-in-process
but there's no space to work.

The more material you have, the more
you can work. Is that true?

You've Seen this Situation, Haven't You?

These are scenes we often find in any production workplace. Photographs of your own plant will probably look similar. Five common characteristics are:

- The plant is large with wide aisles.
- There are many shelves and storage areas.
- There is too much inventory.
- Too many things require transporting.
- Most people don't care about production.

The manufacturing system serves customers through its products. It's desirable, therefore, that service be integrated into the products while at the plant.

The results of a factory revolution in JIT improvement is on-time customer delivery of quality products to the customers when they are needed.

JIT Structure

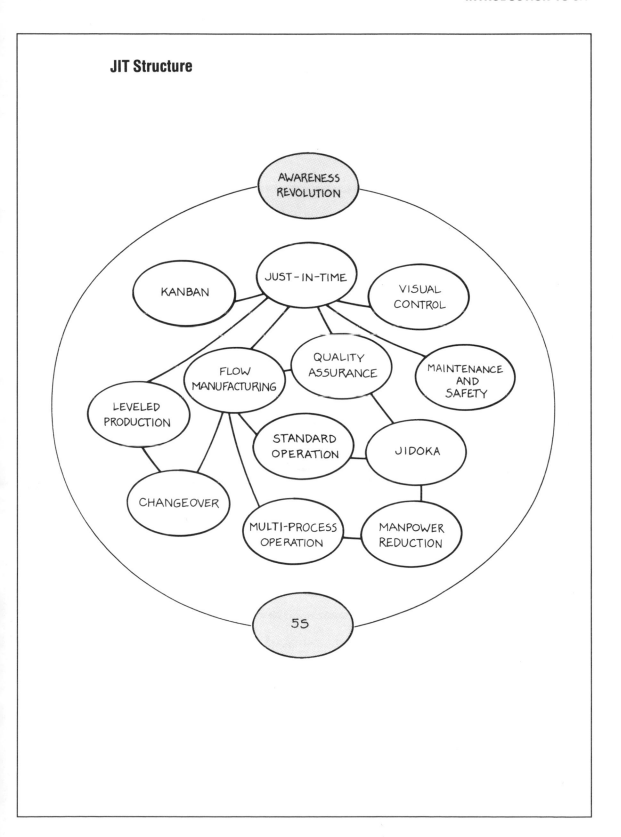

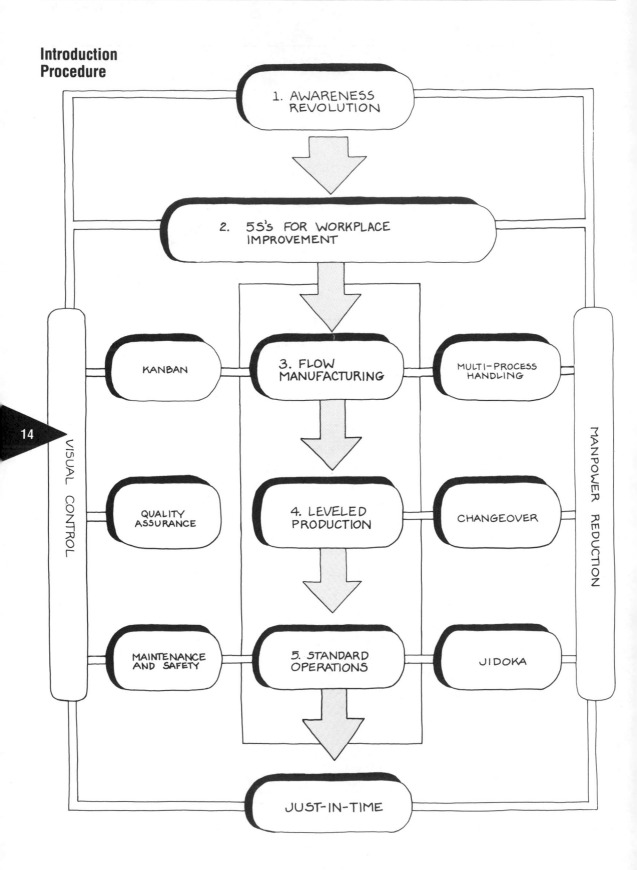

1. Awareness revolution

- Throw out old concepts and turn to the JIT way of thinking.

2. 5S's

- The basics for JIT improvement are the 5S's.

3. Flow manufacturing

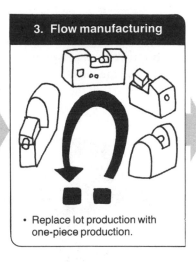

- Replace lot production with one-piece production.

4. Leveled production

- Build products in equal quantities, one at a time, if possible.

5. Standard operations

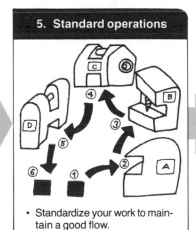

- Standardize your work to maintain a good flow.

JIT

- JIT means "just-in-time."
- Its objective is to produce goods needed by customers economically, quickly, and safely.

Improvement at a Glance

- "Improvement at a glance" means making improvements the moment you find the waste.
- By correcting the situation on the spot, there's no time to spend money.
- This is the key to cost-free improvement.

Before improvement:
Individual machines are
arranged for lot production
— a job-shop layout or design.

5 minutes later: The cellular
manufacturing system concept
is explained to everyone
along with the goals of
one-piece flow manufacturing.

10 minutes later: With
everyone working
together, the layout
change is begun.
Look! We can see how
difficult it is to move
the equipment without
casters.

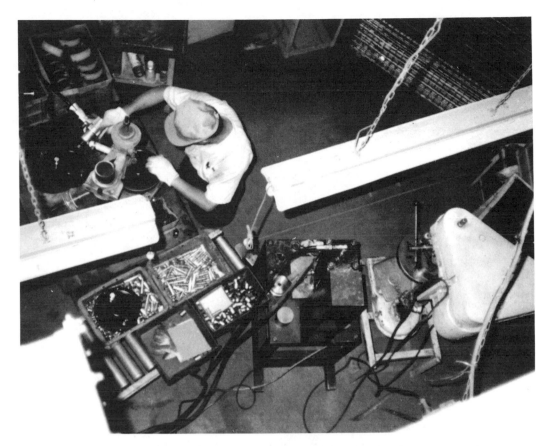

25 minutes later: One worker can run three processes within the cell. This is called multi-process handling. With this design, one-piece flow manufacturing is possible.

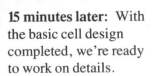

15 minutes later: With the basic cell design completed, we're ready to work on details.

20 minutes later: Having changed the layout into a cell, we must now find out if goods flow smoothly.

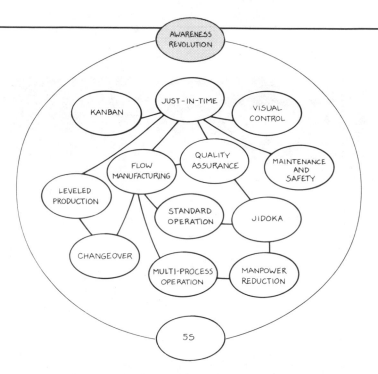

2. Awareness Revolution

Awareness revolution means...

Throwing away traditional attitudes and switching to a JIT way of thinking.

Points:

1. Assume the current production system is the worst.
2. As leader of the revolution within the company, the president must change his or her own way of thinking.
3. To instill a new corporate culture, managers and foremen must work hard to vitalize the entire workplace.
4. Operators must learn new methods. Morning and evening meetings and in-house seminars are needed to retrain the workers.
5. All revolutions and changes encounter resistance. It will be important to have clear policies and principles.

Ten Principles for Improvement

1. Throw out traditional concepts of manufacturing methods.
2. Think of how the new method *will* work — not how it won't.
3. Don't accept excuses. Totally deny the status quo.
4. Don't seek perfection. A 50-percent implementation rate is fine as long as it's done on the spot.
5. Correct mistakes the moment they're found.
6. Don't spend money on improvements.
7. Problems give you a chance to use your brain.
8. Ask "why?" five times.
9. The ideas of ten people are better than the knowledge of one person.
10. Improvement knows no limits.

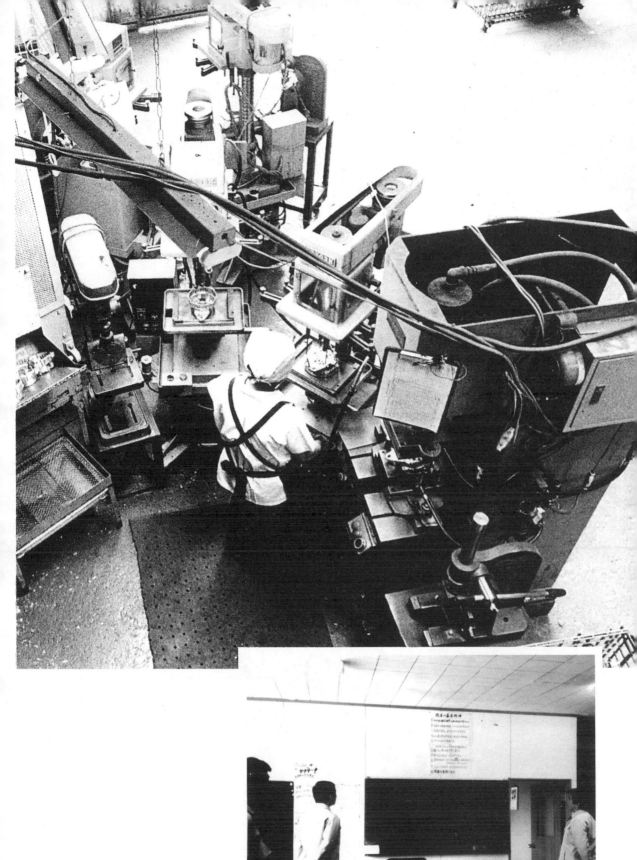

Just-In-Time

Farewell to lot production

- No longer can we sell everything we make.
- It's necessary to produce salable goods quickly.
- Just-in-time is essential for that.
- JIT doesn't mean simply to produce in time.
- Producing *just* in time matters more.

Lot production

Unneeded goods...
In unneeded quantities...
At unneeded times...

Traditional lot production: Lot production was common practice everywhere, the assumption being that products would be sold one way or another. It was felt that having fewer changeovers was better.

JIT production methods: This line produces as quickly as possible products which have been sold. The photograph shows operators standing at a line of machines. Note also that the machines are on casters.

JIT — one-piece flow manufacturing

Needed goods . . .
In needed quantities . . .
At needed times . . .

The JIT production system completely eliminates waste

Work in motion: This woman is carrying packaging materials from the supply area for automotive service parts. This is considered part of her job.

Waste of motion:

- counting things
- moving boxes
- transporting goods
- preparation time
- waiting
- producing defects
- overproduction
- switching things on
- handling materials

Operation = Motion (Waste) + Work (Added Value)

Motion and Work

What is "added value" in operations?

- We operate for 8 hours daily.
- This doesn't mean we actually work 8 hours.
- Operations consist of motion and work.
- Motion alone is a waste that adds cost.
- Work produces the added value customers are willing to pay for.

Operations at work: In this machining process, value is added when the machine is cutting (that is, when the machine is working). In this photograph, the machine is adding value. The operator is not seen because he is elsewhere within the cell performing other value-adding tasks while the machine is running untended.

Surface Improvement vs. Real Improvement

Surface improvement does not eliminate waste.
- There is surface improvement and real improvement.
- If the manufacturing system has large inventories, we probably first consider erecting shelves to hold them.
- If we find a lot of material handling is required, we probably will consider bringing in automated conveyors.
- These are surface improvements (non-value adding).
- The result will still be a lot of inventory and transporting.
- This is not improvement in any real sense.

Material handling by AGVs and AS/RSs: These photographs show an automated storage and retrieval system (AS/RS) and automated guided vehicles (AGV). These systems probably cost thousands of dollars. The question is whether it was really necessary to automate material handling.

Reducing material handling by the arrangement of the machines: The design of the manufacturing system can eliminate the need for costly material handling systems. This machining shop for automobile compressor parts shows a U-shaped cell with three NC machines and several single-function machines. One-at-a-time part transporting is required within the cell. Machines are single-cycle automatics working independently of the operators who walk around the cell.

- For real improvement, we must first ask *why* when encountering any waste.
- *Why* does inventory occur?
- *Why* must we transport goods?
- Ask *why* five times and then think *how* to improve it.
- We call this "5W1H Improvement."

A heavy-duty machine before process improvement: This is a machine for shotblasting automobile parts. It stands three times taller than the average worker and requires a room to itself. The minimum quantity processed at a time is 500, out of which 50 are defective and require an inspector to sort them out. This, in reality, is (1) mass-producing defects and (2) an example of a super machine, something to be avoided.

Procedure for Improving Productivity and Eliminating Waste

Improving the process should be the last step in improvement.

- Steps for improvement are:
  1. Change our way of thinking
  2. Improve the design of the manufacturing system
  3. Improve the processes
- We will never succeed by improving facilities before redesigning the manufacturing system into cells.
- Process improvement requires a lot of money, so we can't afford a mistake here.
- First improve the manufacturing system through JIT production.
- This will tell us which process needs improvement because bottleneck processes and problems become apparent. Then we can improve it.

A small machine after operations improvement: This small part-washing machine was installed between the processes within the cell. Washing parts used to be a separate process done on large lots with an air blower. Now it's done in-process with no noise and requiring very little labor. The machine cost them the price of a bowl of noodle soup.

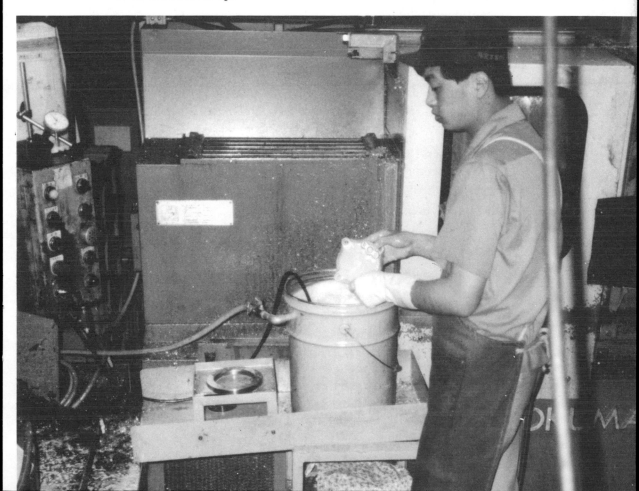

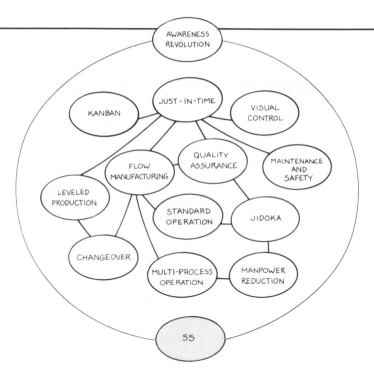

3. The 5S's

Proper arrangement *(Seiri)* . . .
- Sort through, then sort out.
- Sort through what you have, identify what you need, and discard what is unnecessary.

Orderliness *(Seiton)* . . .
- Set things in order.
- Assign a separate location for all essential items. Make the space self-explanatory so everyone knows what goes where.

Cleanliness *(Seiso)* . . .
- Clean equipment, tools, and workplace.
- Keep the workplace spotless at all times.

Cleanup *(Seiketsu)* . . .
- Maintain equipment and tools.
- Keep the workplace clean.

Discipline *(Shitsuke)* . . .
- Stick to the rules scrupulously.
- Make them a habit.

Points:
1. Proper arrangement *(seiri)* and orderliness *(seiton)* must be visual so everyone knows what is where.
2. The 5S's must be a company-wide program.
3. The 5S's are the start in identifying problems and wastes. They must be part of a total improvement program.

PROPER ARRANGEMENT

ORDERLINESS

CLEANLINESS

CLEANUP

DISCIPLINE

FACTORY

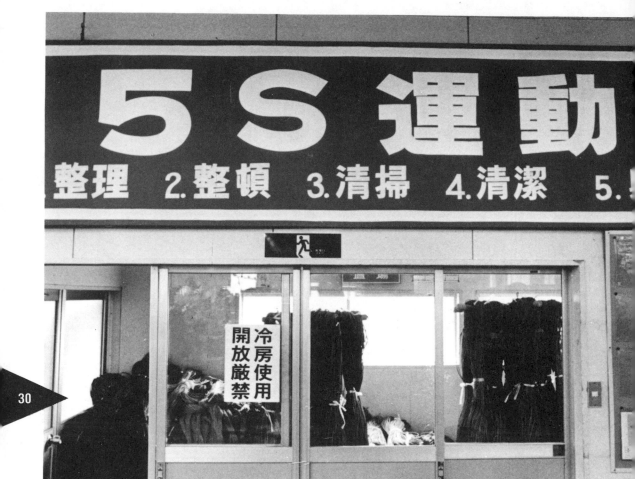

Slogans

This plant's primary product is wire harnesses. They began improvement activities three months ago. Their basis for improvement is the 5S's. Operations improvement is well underway. Work-in-process inventory has been cut in half.

You don't often see such a large 5S slogan hanging in the workplace.

Location	Check Items	Contents
Outside the building	Are there unnecessary items?	Outside
	Are locations specified?	Pallets Materials storage Parts receiving area Trash Storage boxes
	Is the passageway specified?	Are there white and yellow lines? Traffic signs? No exposed cables and wires?
	Is it clean?	Ashtrays, trash, yard, entrance, windows, sidewalks
Offices	Are there unnecessary things?	Posters, papers, halls
	Are locations specified?	Fire extinguisher, first-aid kit
	Is it clean?	Walls clean? Dust on window sills? Windows clean? Flowers?
	Offices	Unnecessary objects on desks? Papers piled up on desks? Nothing under the desks? Designated area for stationery? Telephones not ringing more than three times? Are you sitting straight? Unnecessary papers in the lockers? Designated areas for papers in the lockers? Trash bins and chairs in the aisles? Desks, ashtrays, and floors clean?
	Conference rooms	Unnecessary things? Chairs and desks in designated areas? Tables, ashtrays, and floor clean? Unnecessary posters?
	Bathrooms	Unnecessary things? Enough soap and paper? Basins and floor clean? No graffiti?

Running a Red Tag Campaign

Visual control

Red tags are normally put on regular-sized paper. This reduces costs and makes them easy to read.

We call these red-bordered sheets "red tags."

These red tags describe at a glance the status of wastes accumulating in the plant.

Red tags are concerned with:

Inventory: All inventories including materials, parts, work-in-process, and finished goods.
Equipment: Machine tools, processes, carts, hand trucks, pallets, jigs, tools, cutters, dies, chairs, desks, fork lift trucks, and fixtures.
Space: Floors, aisles, shelves, and warehouses.

Red tag action		
Classification	1. Processes 2. Jigs and tools 3. Inspection devices 4. Raw materials, supplies 5. Parts 6. Work-in-process	7. Subassemblies 8. Finished products 9. Products needing rework 10. Forms like operations sheets 11. Documents
Name		
Number		
Quantity		
Reasons	1. Unnecessary	2. Defective 3. Not urgent
Department	Section	
Date	1. Month	2. Day

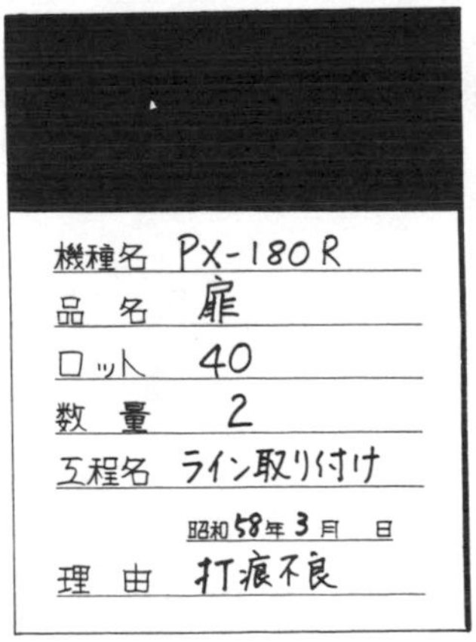

機種名 PX-180R
品　名　扉
ロット　40
数　量　2
工程名　ライン取り付け
昭和 58 年 3 月　日
理　由　打痕不良

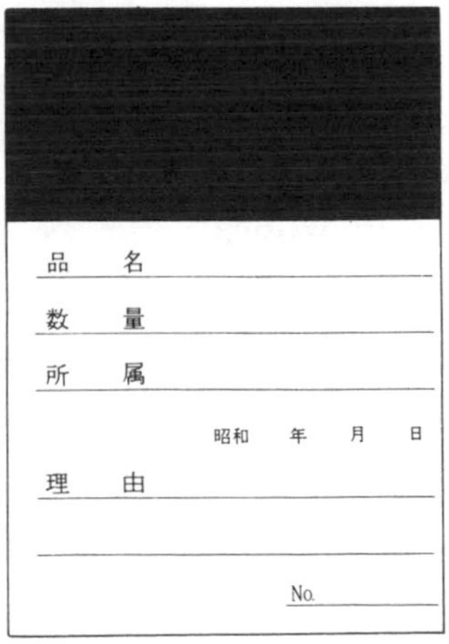

品　名
数　量
所　属
昭和　年　月　日
理　由
No.

Running a Red Tag Campaign

Visual control

- It looks like inventory increased while no one was looking.
- Under the "red tag" program, areas such as this will have a number of red tags.
- Oddly enough, messy plants tend to have more signs that say *seiri* and *seiton*.
- Proper arrangement and orderliness require action and doing — not talking or writing.

Lockers for things that aren't confidential should not have doors. Although this locker originally was intended to keep the workplace in order, we can see what happened. Workers began storing unused things in the locker turning it into a trash container. To sort the needed from the unneeded items, we attached red tags. There are now red sheets everywhere in this locker.

Keeping Shelves in Order

Shelves for storing cosmetic samples showing quality standards

- These shelves hold samples of quality standards used in a cosmetics factory.
- The samples are used in inspection processes on the processing lines.
- The shelves are numbered so everyone can see what is where.
- Everyone seems to follow the procedure.

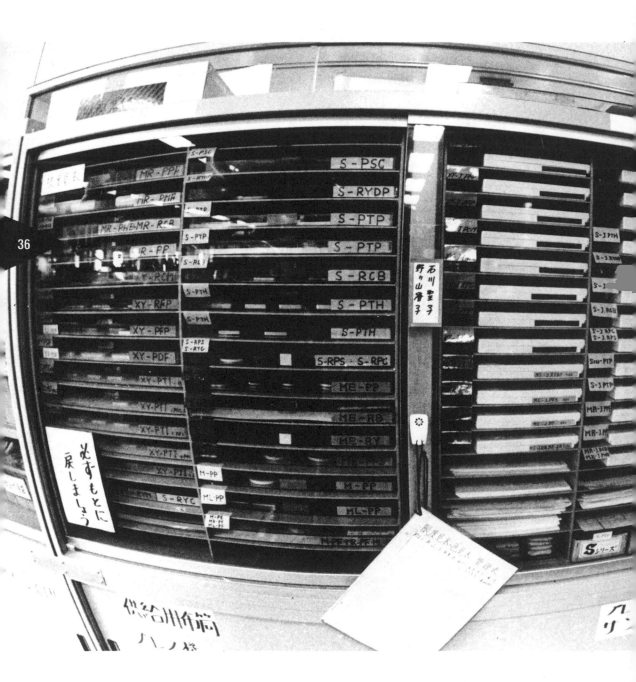

Shelves on the side of the cosmetic line: There are different ways to implement the 5S's. Using boxes is one method. It's also good to group things.

Keeping Shelves in Order

Shelves for electronic parts: Part numbers are clearly indicated. The rules are followed here, which is good. But is there a way to do it without boxes?

Parts shelves: Although many workplaces are orderly, it is rare to see this. These signs clearly indicate the quantity to be moved to the line. Good!

Shelves for wire harnesses

- This is a nice photograph.
- Even small mistakes can be seen clearly.
- It's important to make shelves self-explanatory.
- But it's even more important to make the smallest problems visible to everyone.
- That's 5S!

Keeping Shelves in Order

Electronics parts shelves: The quality of electronic parts assembly is determined in the picking up of component parts. So each part must be easily accessible. That's why we have to consider the best way to keep them orderly.

Ready-made shelves make it difficult to store items of different shapes and sizes. Space is wasted when we try to put everything on them. Handmade shelves might help. Improvement requires creativity.

Shelves for electronics parts

- A manufacturing plant must be flexible.
- Movable shelves arranged by product type are part of the JIT way of thinking.
- What about the parts shelves?
- These shelves are on casters and can be moved any time, to any place.
- Floor layout can be easily changed.

These shelves hold a wide variety of parts. The parts stored on the shelves are indicated by the part numbers on the plates attached to the side of the shelves. The plates must be kept in order so the parts are not lost.

Keeping Shelves in Order

- One improvement rule is to not spend money.
- The same goes for the 5S's.
- This example shows a medical supply company.
- They made shelves for jigs and tools using cardboard.
- They have many different jigs and tools such as screwdrivers and clippers.
- They're light enough for cardboard shelves.

Visual orderliness of jigs: These are shelves for jigs used in changeovers at the cosmetics plant. Jigs used in their assembly lines are placed in separate boxes. Frequently used jigs are placed usually right beside the machine. All the shelves and cases are clearly labeled so anyone can return tools to their proper places. Looking for changeover tools is considered part of changeover time. The basics of changeover are the 5S's.

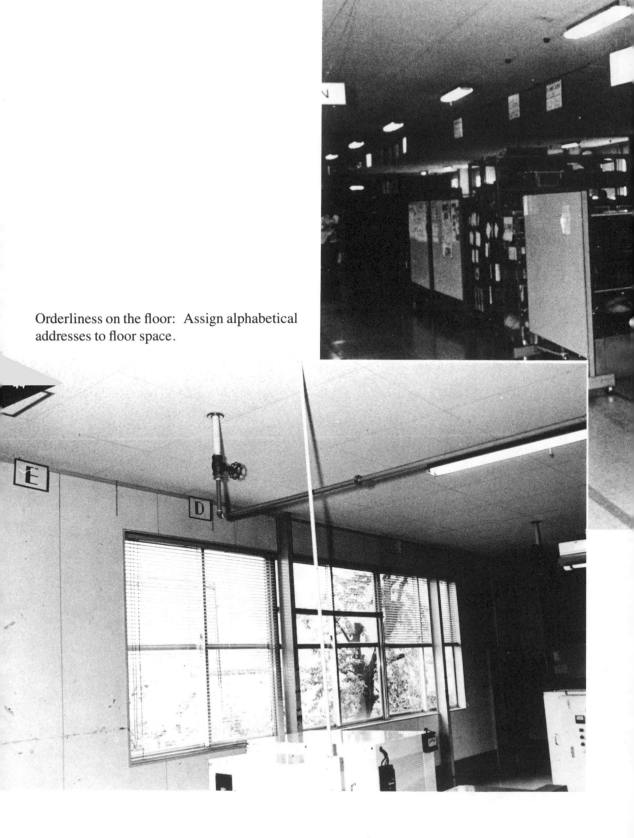

Orderliness on the floor: Assign alphabetical addresses to floor space.

Keeping Storage Areas in Order

Materials storage

- How can these boxes be handled?
- That's an important point of the 5S's.
- Don't let them accumulate.
- Even though there are still a lot of boxes, it's better than it used to be!

Keeping the Workplace in Order

Hand trucks

- The 5S's say, "Keep the place in order!"
- They also say, "Don't place anything directly on the floor."
- In this plant everything is placed on wheeled hand trucks or wheeled pallets.
- They protect the floor and are easy to move.

The location of carts is clearly indicated. There seems to be no unauthorized parking.

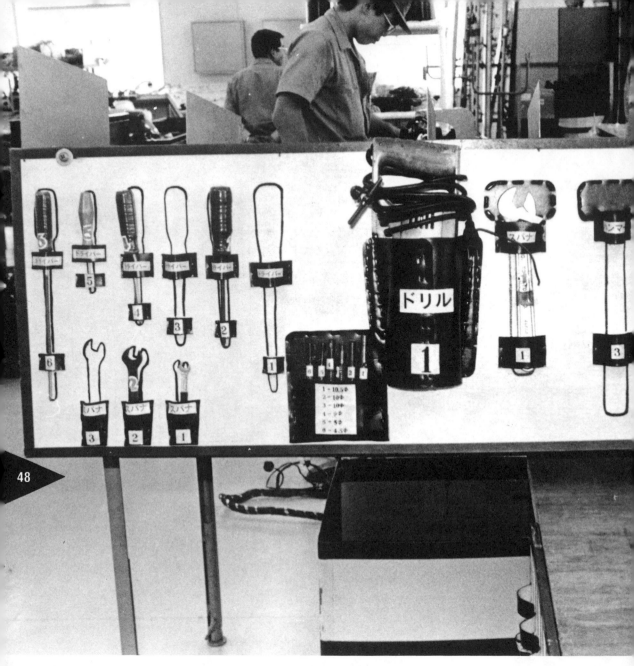

48

Keeping the Workplace in Order

Hand tools

- This photograph illustrates the basics for a tool board.
- The tool is easy to pick up.
- It's easy to put back.
- We must consider where to place frequently used tools.
- The most important thing is that workers find the board easy to use.

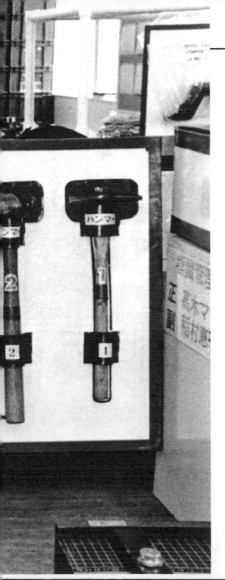

Outline the shapes of the tools on the board so everyone knows what goes where and what tools are in use. How could we make it easy to identify who is using the tools?

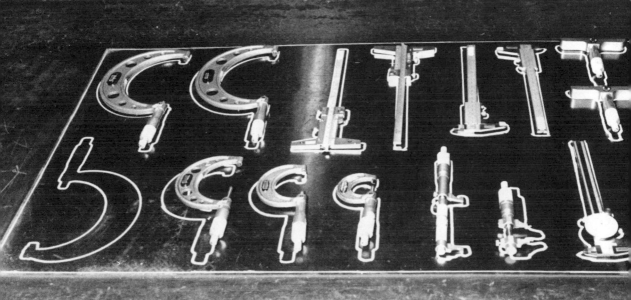

Keeping the Workplace in Order

Utility closet

- The first step in the 5S's is storing cleaning tools properly.
- Dust pans should be hung properly.
- Then, arrange the inside of the closet.
- If the closet has a door, it tends to become messy inside.

Keep cleaning tools in order: Most cleaning tools get dirty. Those that do should be placed where they can be seen by everyone. Placed as in the photograph, they tell everyone when they need to be cleaned and we always have clean tools to use.

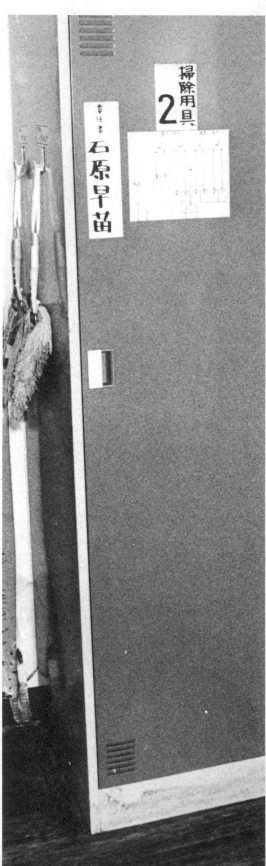

This looks pretty good!

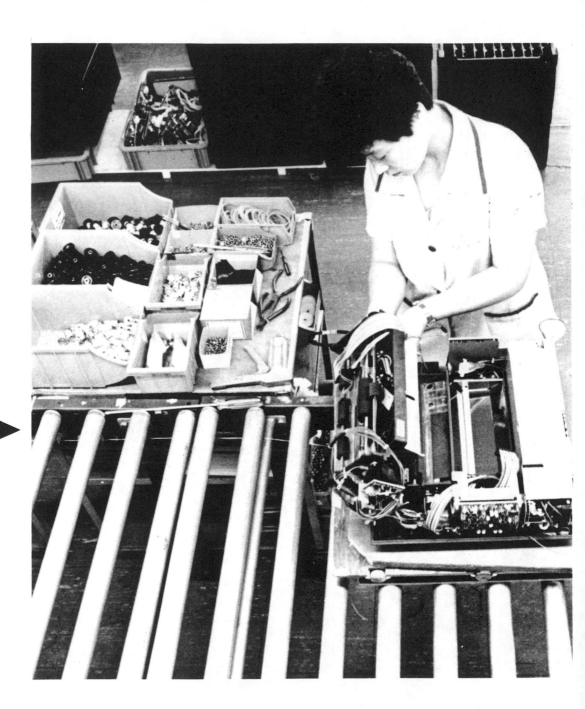

52

Keeping Worktables in Order

FAX assembly table

- When determining the location of parts in the process, the first thing to consider is how easy it is for workers to pick them up.
- Eliminate wasted motions.
- To do this, consider carefully even the smallest part — such as a nut.
- Arrange the parts in order of the work sequence.

This plant's assembly line has a good layout. Assemblers have parts within easy reach.

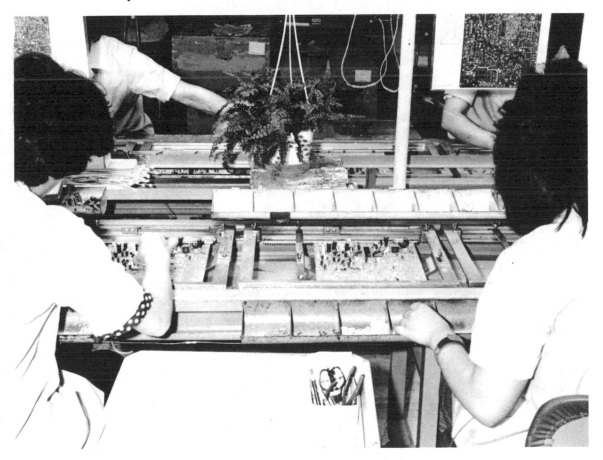

Keeping Worktables in Order

Assembly table for cardiac monitors

To locate small parts such as nuts and washers, plastic swizzle sticks can be used. The nuts and washers are easy to pick off the sticks. The sticks are inexpensive.

This is a VCR assembly shop. Needed parts are located within the worker's reach — perfect placement.

Keeping the Office in Order

Paper

- Apply the 5S's to the office.
- Lots of supplies and paper are used in a manufacturing company.
- Keep them in order.
- Treat office supplies like any other materials or supplies. Inventory is waste!
- Through this company's 5S office activities, stationery was removed from individual desks.
- They collected a year's worth of inventory from the desks alone!
- They haven't purchased any stationery since.

This office doesn't have individual desks. Large worktables are shared by several people.

Keeping the Office in Order

Files

- Paper and paper forms are used everywhere!
- Think of production manuals and other documents.
- Apply the 5S's here,too!
- Paper takes up a lot of space. It's heavy and frequently not used.
- Let's throw it away.
- We never look at 90 percent of the papers in our desks anyway.
- This office has no individual desks and files.

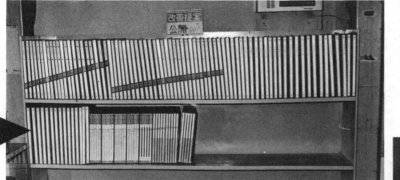

By filing suggestion sheets, workers can see them any time. The notebooks are numbered and the numbers form a sloped line so anyone can return one to the right place.

The desks are bare. We might think no one worked today. But they did. The improvement applied here is that everyone clears his or her desk before going home. The two still working are planning people . . .

Cleanup

Everyone should dispose of trash.

- Workers as well as machines create trash.
- Try not to produce any.
- If trash is unavoidable, dispose of it at once.
- We often see trash strewn around a bin.
- The worker in the photograph attacked this problem creatively.

Disposing of chips: Many machines produce waste materials. It's important to control this in some way. We're behind the times if we still sweep the floors.

Rest areas

- The 5S's and operations improvement created the extra space in this plant.
- In this example, the space along the line is used as a rest area.
- Everyone contributed — so everyone can use it!

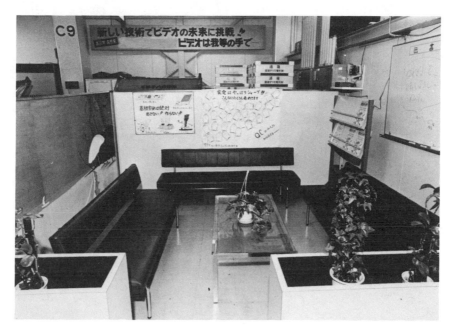

Rest areas are often left noticeably messy with food, cigarette butts, and paper. We must keep these common areas clean for everyone.

Factories are too big for the 5S's to be conducted by any one person. We need everyone to communicate and cooperate with coworkers even if it means having a discussion with a manager we dislike. It would be nice to have a place where we could feel at home communicating with people. Good 5S ideas are usually born there.

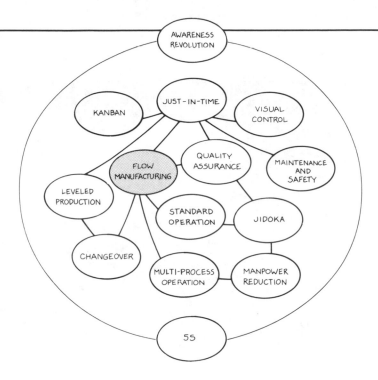

4. Flow Manufacturing

Flow manufacturing is...

Producing one piece at a time following the sequence and rules of the cycle time.

Points:

1. Place machines in the process sequence.
2. Design the cell in a U-shape.
3. Make one piece at a time within the cell.
4. Train workers to handle more than one process.
5. Produce according to the cycle time.
6. Have the operators work standing up and walking.
7. Use slower, dedicated machines that are smaller and less expensive.

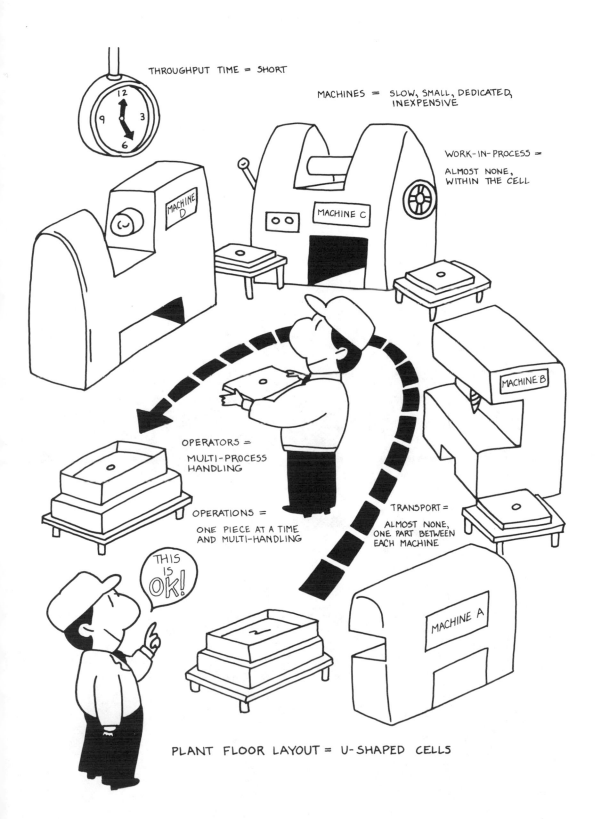

THROUGHPUT TIME = SHORT

MACHINES = SLOW, SMALL, DEDICATED, INEXPENSIVE

WORK-IN-PROCESS = ALMOST NONE, WITHIN THE CELL

MACHINE D

MACHINE C

MACHINE B

OPERATORS = MULTI-PROCESS HANDLING

OPERATIONS = ONE PIECE AT A TIME AND MULTI-HANDLING

TRANSPORT = ALMOST NONE, ONE PART BETWEEN EACH MACHINE

THIS IS OK!

MACHINE A

PLANT FLOOR LAYOUT = U-SHAPED CELLS

Lot Production vs. Flow Manufacturing

A comparison

- Traditional floor layout was of the job-shop type.
- Machines of the same type were grouped together.
- This, however, prevents flow manufacturing.
- The first step to flow manufacturing is to create something more compatible to subassembly and final assembly lines.
- This is the cell.

Lot production: This is the inspection area of an automobile factory. It's not a warehouse but look at all the inventory! After the parts are machined, they are inspected lot by lot.

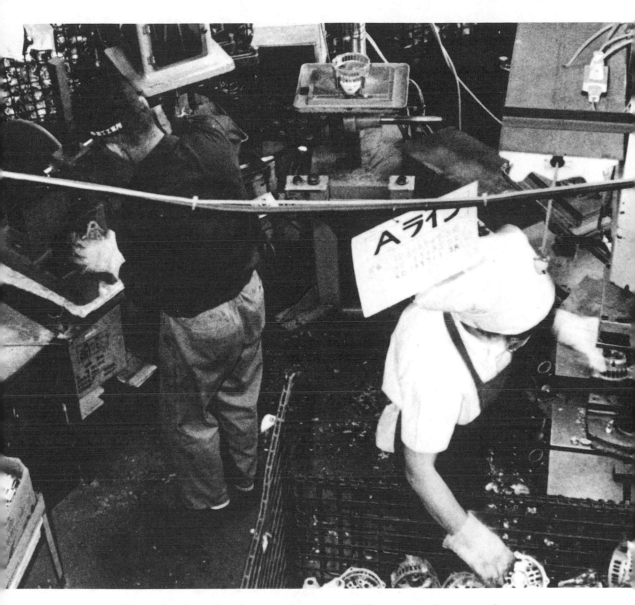

This is an example of a manufacturing cell for automotive parts. One operator handles seven processes.

Change the design of the manufacturing system to U-shaped cells. Then institute one-part-at-a-time manufacturing within the cell, instead of lot production.

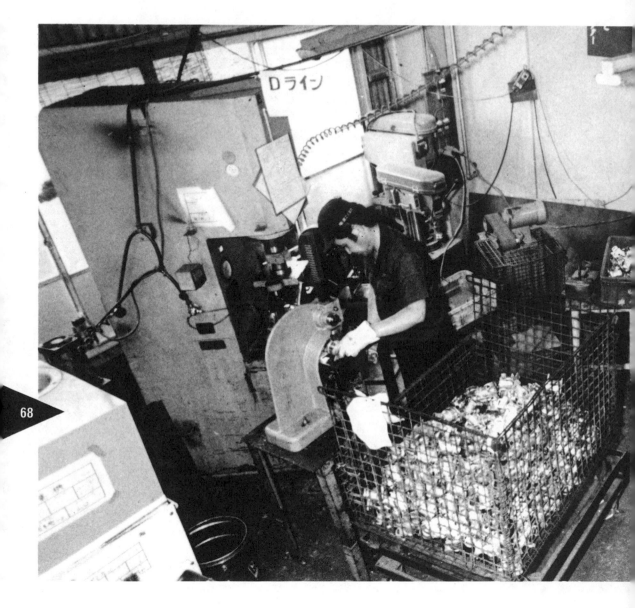

Cellular Shop

Machining cell for finishing automobile diecastings

- This is the machining cell for finishing automobile diecastings.
- Machines used to be in a job-shop layout.
- A cellular layout was developed which included a small, dedicated shot blasting machine for deburring the parts. Parts are processed one part at a time. The machine replaces the larger, heavy-duty machine shown on page 26. The machines are placed in line according to the process sequence, forming a cell.
- In the job shop, inventory used to stack up between processes.

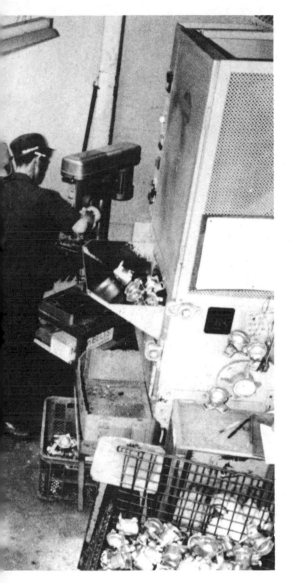

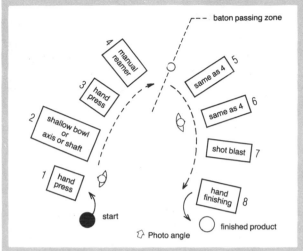

A manufacturing cell manned by two workers running eight processes arranged in a U-shaped cell. One worker operates processes 1-4. The second worker operates processes 5-8. The first worker hands off work to the second worker in the relay zone.

Arrange machines according to processing sequence.

Instead of grouping machines together by type in one place in what is called a "job shop," arrange them according to the process sequence, moving the machines in-line. Attach casters when possible to machines and worktables to make them easily mobile. U-shaped manufacturing cells are the basic building blocks of cellular manufacturing systems.

- It was difficult to meet needed quantities because of the high number of defectives produced. Materials were not inspected prior to the finishing process.
- Dramatically shortened throughput times now make it possible to correct defectives quickly.
- This cell's main job is deburring. It creates a lot of dirt. The tasks before them now are to pursue the 5S's and synchronize the diecasting process with the finished cell.

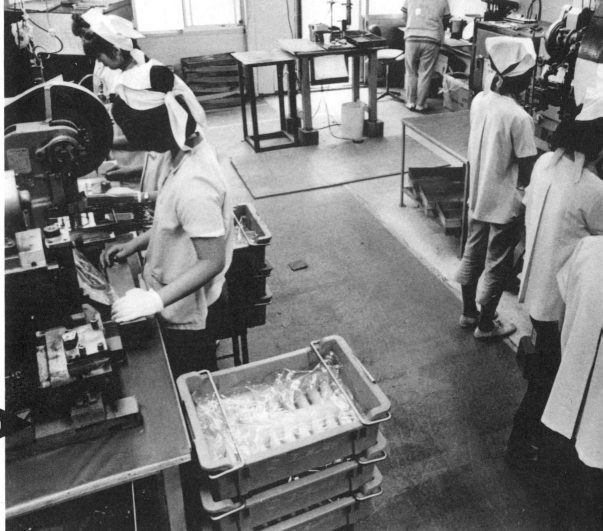

U-Shaped Line

Automotive electronics parts line

- This is an automotive electronics parts assembly line.
- It was once based on large quantities of work in process. (See the box at the bottom of the photograph.)
- Throughput times were long.
- Workers became nervous trying to keep up with production requirements — specified production rates.
- Inventory no longer piles up between processes. There is a smooth one-piece-at-a-time flow from raw materials to finished product.
- These changes required a minimum monetary investment.
- The number of workers, in fact, was reduced as the line became flexible enough to assign operators according to quantities needed.
- The workers walk from machine to machine around the cell.

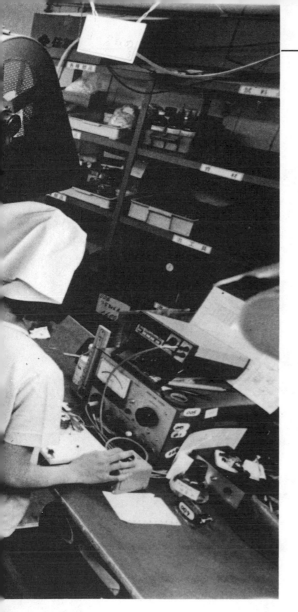

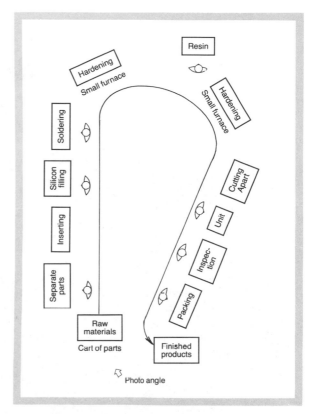

Layout of a U-shaped assembly line

- What's the best design of a manufacturing system for processing?
- A straight line is OK — but it requires operators to walk back to the beginning of the line to start. This is wasted movement.
- A U-shaped line can solve this problem.

- Productivity improved.
- This photograph shows the model — the company's first U- shaped line. At first, workers resisted the idea because they were no longer able to work sitting down. However, results will show that other lines must follow suit.

U-Shaped Line

Basic board assembly line

- This is the line for packaging the printed circuit boards used in cardiac monitors.
- Workers used to sit in specific locations surrounded by parts.
- The general disorder in supplying parts made for many exceptions and rush orders.
- Productivity was low.
- Now carrying five or six different parts, workers walk around the cell installing parts into the printed circuit boards.
- This made it possible to establish one complete cell to do everything from laying out parts, to soldering, to leadcutting, to touch-up.
- This dramatically reduced work-in-process inventory.
- Productivity has already increased 50 percent and they're just beginning.

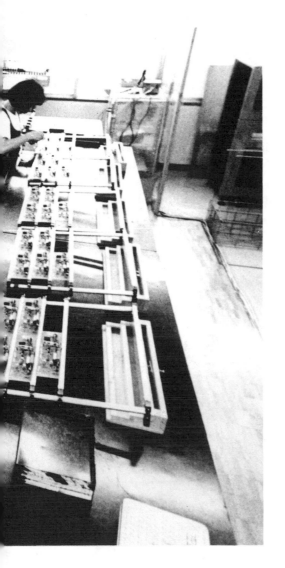

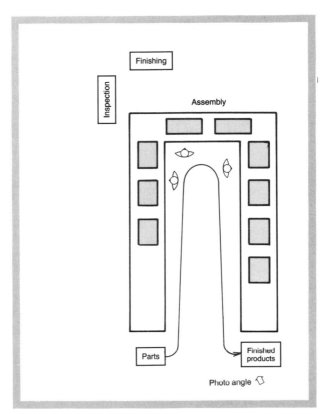

Finishing

Inspection

Assembly

Parts

Finished products

Photo angle

Design of a manned assembly cell for assembling printed circuit boards.

Cellular Manufacturing and Assembly

Sensor assembly line

- This U-shaped line assembles sensors.
- All workers stand except pregnant women and those performing specially designated jobs.
- Here harnesses are measured and cut, and sensor parts installed.
- Although inspection (at the end) is performed in lots, one-piece flow manufacturing has been achieved in the six previous processes.
- The epoxy application and hardening stages which follow the inspection process will be added to the cell.
- Everyone is working hard to bring improvements to the processes following inspection.

One-piece flow in the cell

- Don't process every piece in a lot before sending it on to the next process.
- It's best to process one piece at a time.
- Work flows like a bamboo leaf boat bobbing down a river.

Assembly cell with seven stations.

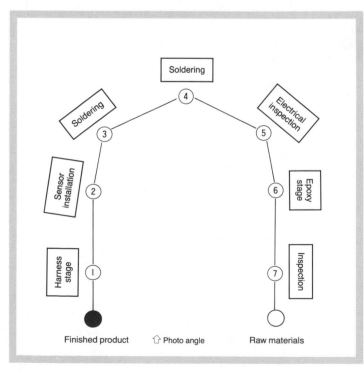

When the worker is standing to perform a task, it is necessary to raise the table height. Wooden or concrete blocks are placed under the table legs.

Multi-Process Handling

Assembly line for cardiac monitors

- This is an assembly line for cardiac monitors.
- In the old design, the workers used to sit at the assembly station.
- Each worker was assigned a single job. Consequently, work-in-process piled up between processes.
- Lot production was used. Many defectives were discovered at the final electric inspection.
- Now they have a U-shaped assembly cell making one piece at a time. (See sketch on right.)
- Products are tested individually at the final electric inspection process. Problems are solved quickly.
- There used to be no space available for a rest area.
- The new design reduced the floor space needed for this assembly line, creating room for the rest area shown on the right.
- Most workers are part-time and didn't mind standing. They were trained to handle multiple processes.

Multi-process handling by multi-skilled operators

- One operator per machine may create a flow line but does not reduce the number of operators. Training the operators to become multi-skilled and capable of handling several processes will solve the problem.

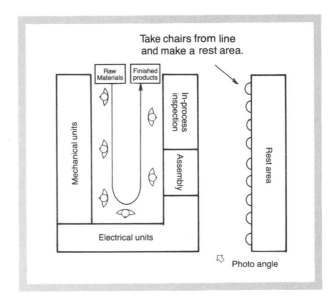

Cycle Time

A line for machining automobile parts

- Machines in this line machine automobile parts.
- These workers used to produce in lots using containers of parts like the one shown in the center of the photograph.
- The concept of "cycle time" did not yet exist.
- Workers only knew to produce, produce, produce!
- They now produce one piece at a time from the raw material stage to finished product, walking from machine to machine.
- Inspection accompanies each process in a line.
- The rule is to never pass defectives to the next process.
- *Poka-yoke* (defect-prevention) devices are used in processes where mistakes tend to be made.
- It was difficult for older workers to get used to standing.
- Doing quality work at all times is important.

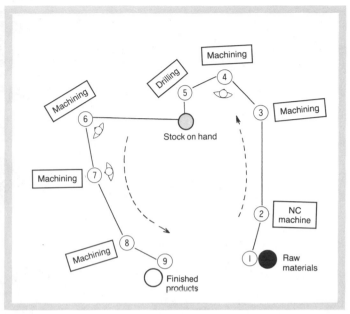

The operator on the right services 2, 3, 4, 5 — see path. The two operators on the left do 6, 7, 8.

Cycle time

- "Cycle time" is the time it takes to carry one part all the way through the cell.
- How to calculate cycle time:

$$\text{Daily Quantity Required} = \frac{\text{Monthly Quantity Needed}}{\text{Working Days per Month}}$$

$$\text{Cycle Time} = \frac{\text{Working Hours per Day}}{\text{Daily Quantity Required}}$$

Poka-yoke

- *Poka* means mistakes caused by carelessness. *Yoke* means to avoid.
- *Poka-yoke* is called "mistake-proofing" in the United States but really means defect prevention.
- A single defect can damage the total credibility of a manufacturer. Zero defects (ZD) is fundamental to cellular manufacturing. Poka-yoke is a system that prevents defects by eliminating defects at the source. (Refer to Shigeo Shingo's book entitled *Zero Quality Control: Source Inspection and the Poka-yoke System* [Cambridge, MA: Productivity Press, 1986].)

Standing (Chair-Free) Operations

VCR assembly line

- This is a VCR assembly line.
- Chairs were removed and workers asked to stand.
- Worktables were raised by placing metal stands under each leg.

A standing (chair-free) operation

- It's not difficult to implement flow manufacturing.
- First, have the workers stand.
- Multiple processes can then be handled while items are assembled one at a time.
- The workers can walk from process to process.

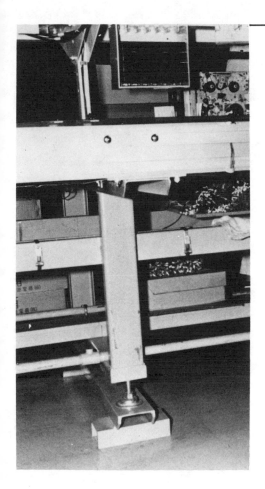

A chair-free operation was begun in this VCR assembly line. The continuous flow line is 90 meters long. The tables were raised using iron angles and blocks of wood.

Standing (Chair-Free) Operations

A telephone equipment line

- This conveyor line assembles telephone equipment.
- Operators used to sit.
- Wooden blocks were placed under the legs to raise the height of the tables.
- We seldom see chair-free conveyor lines.
- Productivity improved 30 percent.

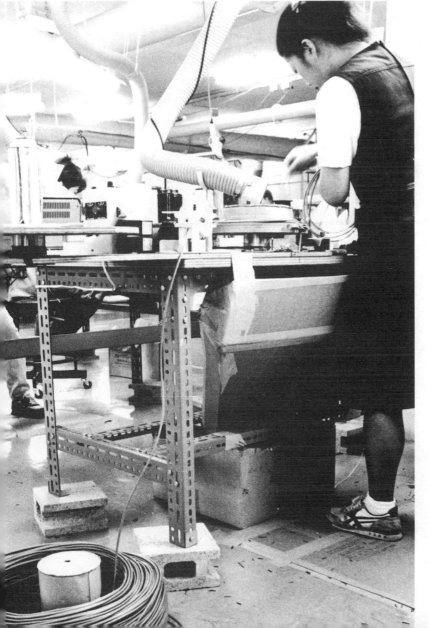

Concrete blocks are used to lift the table.

Relay assembly: Worktables have blocks under their legs.

Standing (Chair-Free) Operations

An Integrated Circuit (IC) insert line

- This is an IC insert line.
- It was once on a track conveyor.
- The conveyor was removed to allow greater flexibility in production.
- Worktables especially made for this operation allow workers to stand while assembling.
- The floor is covered with a rubber mat to reduce fatigue and prevent the buildup of static electricity.

IC insertion — standing

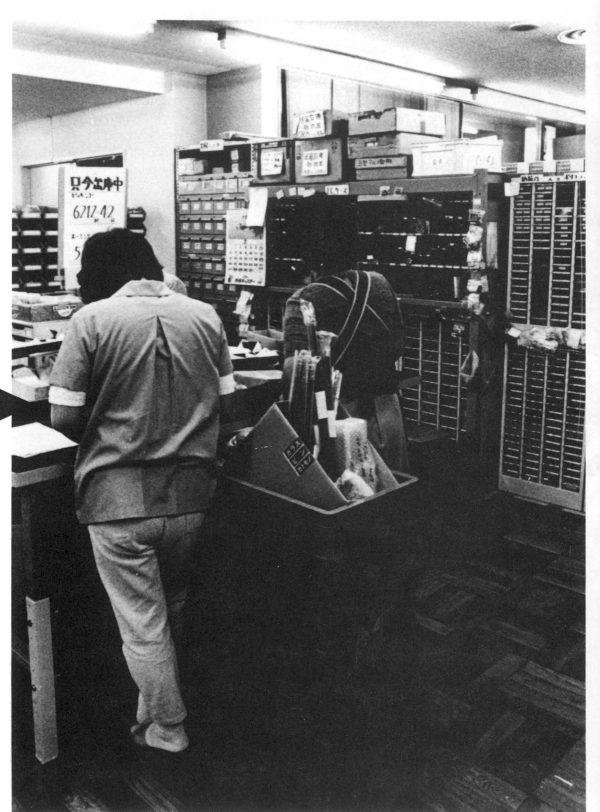

Standing (Chair-Free) Operations

A materials warehouse for electronic parts

- This is a materials warehouse for electronic parts.
- These workers used to work sitting.
- They now stand.
- This created more space.
- Worker movements have improved.
- They are now implementing this type of operation in other areas such as manufacturing and inspection.

These workers are in the materials warehouse. The worktables they use have casters for easy moving.

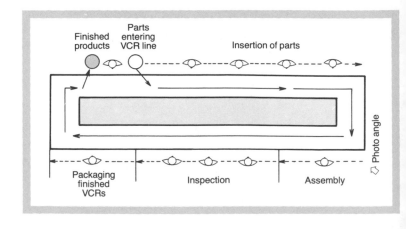

Finished products   Parts entering VCR line   Insertion of parts

Packaging finished VCRs   Inspection   Assembly

Photo angle

Mutual Line Assistance

VCR assembly line

- This is a VCR continuous flow assembly line 90 meters long.
- Workers used to be seated along the line.
- Balancing of work between the stations was so uneven that goods piled up between workers.
- So much inventory was being supplied to each process that the aisles were cluttered with parts.
- Furthermore, shortages of particular parts caused frequent linestops.
- For the first time, chairs were removed and workers stood along the line. This was unique in this area.
- By learning the processes before and after theirs, the workers became multi-skilled. The workforce was reduced by 15 workers.
- Cooperation among workers increased as they became multi-skilled. They were able to adjust to changes in the line speed more easily; that is, they were flexible in meeting line requirements. The number of linestops decreased dramatically.
- The first attempt to implement this design failed. Some workers resisted standing. It took three months to change their way of thinking — but in the end it was implemented successfully.
- Lesson: If time is not allowed for implementation, there is a tendency to fail.

The workers cooperate with and assist each other within the specific areas along the line. In order to balance the station times, some stations have multiple workers while others are multiple process.

Helping each other

Personnel \ Process	A	B	C	D	E	F	G	H
A	O	O	O					
B			O	O	O			
C					O	O	O	
D							O	O
E								

Mutual Line Assistance

Telephone equipment assembly line

- This is a telephone equipment assembly line.
- The workers used to work sitting.
- The previous method was to take the item from the conveyor, process it, and put it back on the conveyor.
- Waste was caused by workers removing too many items at once.
- Workers now assist one another along the line.
- The goal is to make all the workers capable of handling many processes depending on the changes in production quantities.
- This is a new way to operate on conveyor assembly lines.
- Improvements include a timely supply of parts with no waste.
- The next step is to shorten the line by reducing in-process inventories within the line.

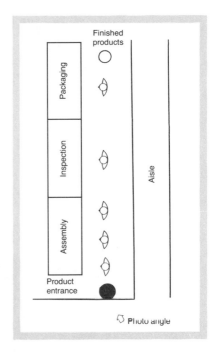

Finished
products

Packaging

Inspection

Aisle

Assembly

Product
entrance

Photo angle

Small In-Line Machines

Small Ultra-Violet (UV) application machine

- This is a sensor assembly process.
- They used to use an epoxy resin coating to mount the sensor.
- Hardening the epoxy took one hour, using heat.
- Because of this long process delay, there was a lot of work-in-process inventory.
- They now use an ultra-violet paint to mount the sensor.
- Hardening takes five to ten seconds in the UV box shown below.
- There is no work-in-process inventory.
- This machine was designed by the operators themselves.

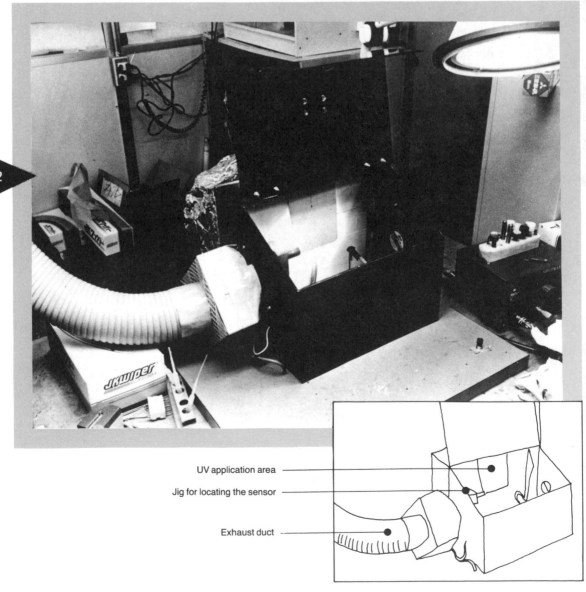

UV application area

Jig for locating the sensor

Exhaust duct

Shot blast equipment

- The larger shot blasting machines needed 300 to 500 parts per machine cycle. Products were often damaged by this large machine.
- Because work was done in large lots, a large work-in-process inventory was needed.
- Together, the workers developed a smaller shot blasting machine that reduced inventory and eliminated damage.
- Parts are processed one at a time.
- These smaller machines can process 10 to 15 parts per hour.
- They are now located along the line, making continuous flow manufacturing possible.

The next product is placed on the holding tray during shot blasting. When the shot blasting is completed, the lower door opens and the finished product drops out into the lower tray. The entrance then opens and the next part is loaded in automatically.

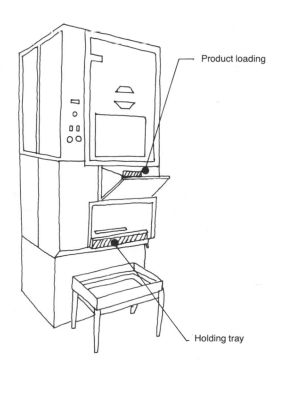

Product loading

Holding tray

Small In-Line Machines

Small soldering machine

- This machine solders electric appliances.
- It automatically fluxes the parts and preheats parts before soldering.
- This equipment is located right in-line with the processes which populate the board with electrical parts.
- It is located next to the electronic part testing process.
- It is synchronized with leadcut, touch-up, and final part installation. The line is designed for one-piece operation.
- There is no work-in-process inventory. This is an example of continuous flow manufacturing from raw materials to final test.
- The machine was made in-house.

Small washing machine

- This is a station in the motor assembly line.
- Excess flux (applied for soldering) is being washed away.
- A large machine used to be used to wash the flux away. The large machine required large lots.
- The operators themselves made a small washing machine and installed it right in the line.
- Continuous flow was now possible.
- Work-in-process here is only the parts being washed in the machine at any given time.

Small In-Line Machines

An example of process delay

- This is the process for drying adhesives.
- There used to be separate workstations for application and drying processes and work-in-process piled up at the drying process.
- Now only one line is used for both application and drying of adhesives.
- Electric fans are used to dry the products naturally.
- Drying time controls the quantity of work-in-process in the dryer.
- Number of Parts in Drying $= \dfrac{\text{Drying time}}{\text{Average Station Time}}$
- The parts are delayed in process to permit the adhesive to cure.

Small dryer

- This is a drying furnace used to dry the adhesive used for a sensor assembly. For maximum efficiency, this large and expensive furnace required that parts be dried in the largest lots possible.
- Workers now use small, inexpensive hair dryers operating at temperatures of 80 degrees C ($\pm$ 5 degrees C). These small dryers satisfy the needs of the process perfectly.
- Lots are as small as possible.

A labeling machine

- This machine labels small motors.
- The labels are detached automatically, one at a time from a sheet of paper.
- The machine was made inexpensively in-house.

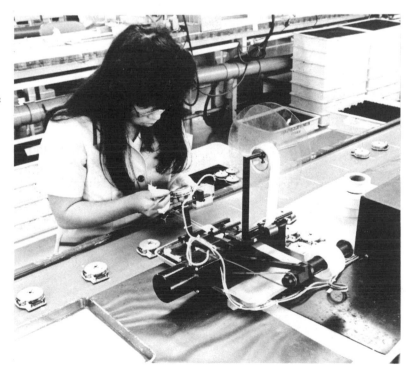

Small In-Line Machines

Jigs to tighten screws

- This is a VCR assembly line.
- This process used to be a bottleneck along the line.
- Workers used to hold the body of the product with the left hand and tighten the screws with the right hand.
- They invented a simple mechanism to hold and locate the screws, freeing both hands for screw tightening.
- Production now flows smoothly at this point on the line.

A small machine to tighten nuts

- This process inserts a washer and hexagonal nuts into a sensor.
- The nuts had to be screwed on by hand and it took 10 seconds to tighten one.
- The work was done in lots.
- Now the work is done one at a time.
- To make the job easier, workers invented a small nut-tightening machine using a revolving rubber wheel from a child's toy.
- When the worker extends his arms to perform the task, the machine senses this movement and automatically begins revolving the wheel.
- All the worker has to do is press a nut against the revolving wheel and it is tightened in one second.
- Prior to this improvement, workers complained about sore hands.

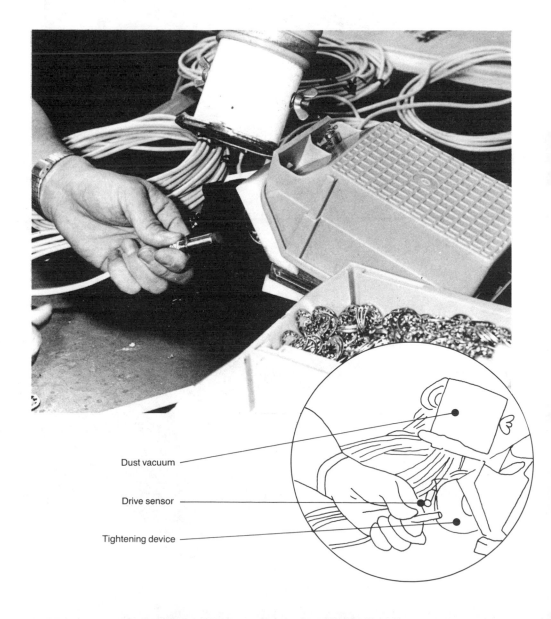

Dust vacuum

Drive sensor

Tightening device

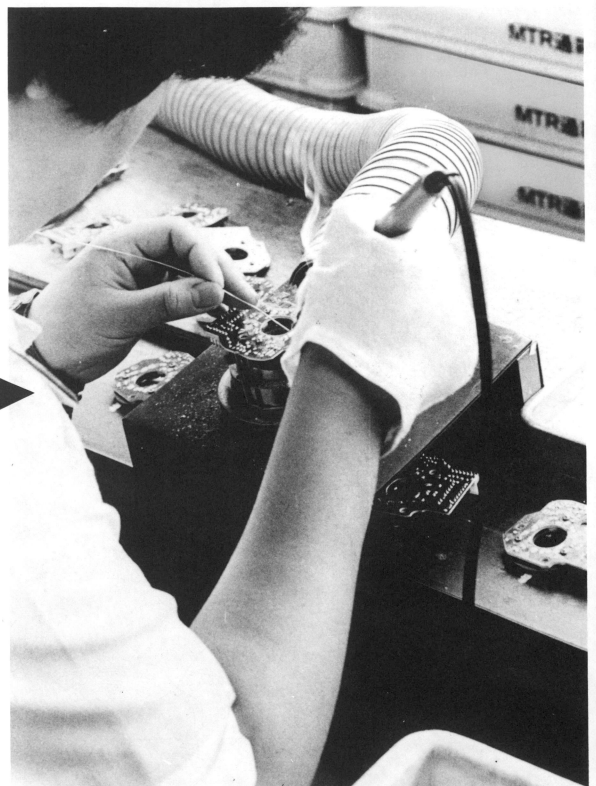

Small In-Line Machines

Ventilation system for soldering

- This is a soldering process.
- Soldering needs a ventilation system.
- This improves efficiency and cleanliness.

Small inexpensive machines

- Large machines should be avoided in lines or cells when possible.
- Multifunctional and high-speed machines are usually not suitable.
- The machine should be inexpensive and dedicated to the parts being made in line or cell.
- The machine should not slow down the production rate of the cell.

We can see a lot of snake-like flexible ducts hanging from the ceiling.

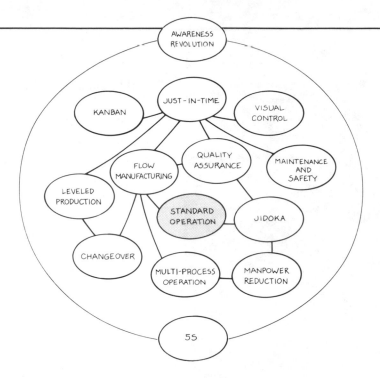

5. Standard Operations

Standard operations mean...

Rules and methods to produce quality products safely and inexpensively by the efficient arrangement of people, products, and machines.

Points:

The three basics of standard operations are:

- Cycle time
- Work sequence (manufacturing and assembly cells)
- Standard stock-on-hand (within the cell)

Use the following operations charts for standardized operations:

- Worktables of parts-production capacity
- Operations pointers
- Standard operations bulletins
- Standard operations routine sheets
- Manuals on work methods

Use these charts to improve and standardize operations.

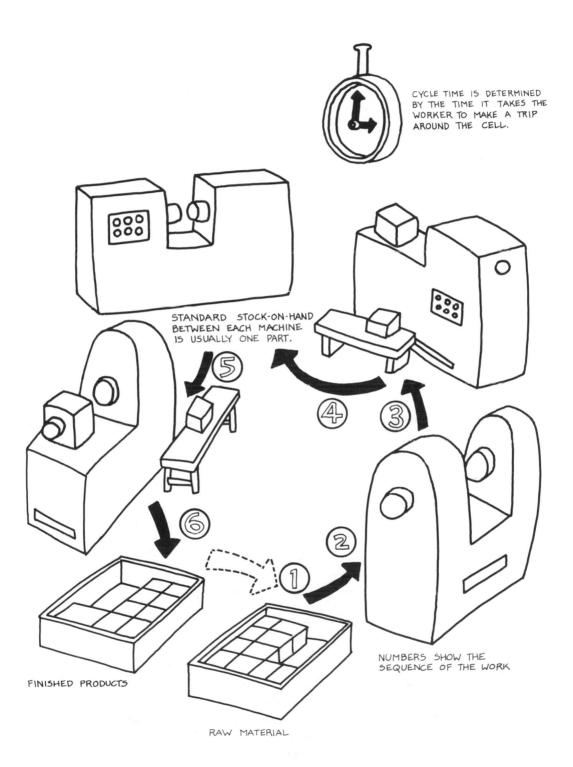

CYCLE TIME IS DETERMINED BY THE TIME IT TAKES THE WORKER TO MAKE A TRIP AROUND THE CELL.

STANDARD STOCK-ON-HAND BETWEEN EACH MACHINE IS USUALLY ONE PART.

NUMBERS SHOW THE SEQUENCE OF THE WORK

FINISHED PRODUCTS

RAW MATERIAL

Operations Charts

Parts-production capacity		Part No.			Model			Group		Date
		Part name			Pieces			Name		
Process name	No.	Basic time			Tool		Process capacity	Remarks		
		Hand-work	Auto-mated work	Comple-tion work	Setups	Setup time				
		Min. | Sec.	Min. | Sec.	Min. | Sec.						
	Total									

This table is used to show the capacity (production rate) of the cell.

Job request		Process name		Name	
		Group		Job description	
No.	Critical factors	Correct/incorrect			

This chart is used to list important points regarding machine settings, tool changing, workpiece loading, unloading, setups (changing the machine over for different parts), and methods of operation.

Work methods table				Part No.		Required No.		Group		Date Approved
				Part name		Breakdown no.		Name		
No.	Job description	Quality		Critical factors	Net time	Cycle time				
		Check	Gage		Min. Sec.	Standard wait time				
						Safety precautions				
						Quality check				
						Net time				
				Total time						

This instructs operators how to follow standard operations and methods.

Standard operations bulletin	Job description	From:	Group	Date Approved
		To:	Name	

This chart indicates machine cell design (the layout), required cycle times, work sequences, and standard inventories. With this chart, we can verify if operations are being followed correctly.

Standard operations in a cosmetics assembly cell

- This is a U-shaped assembly cell. It has two workers.
- The cell is standardized.
- The standard operations routine sheet is posted above the workers' heads. It tells operators about decisions made by managers or group leaders.
- This example of visual control allows people to identify a problem simply by looking at the cell.
- The standard operations routine sheet is used to perfect the operations of the U-shaped cell.

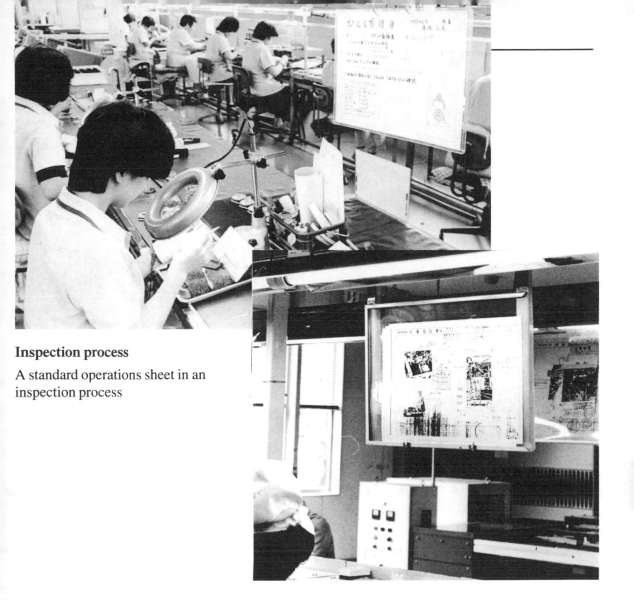

Inspection process

A standard operations sheet in an inspection process

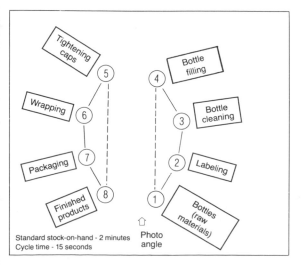

Standard stock-on-hand - 2 minutes
Cycle time - 15 seconds

5 Tightening caps
6 Wrapping
7 Packaging
8 Finished products

4 Bottle filling
3 Bottle cleaning
2 Labeling
1 Bottles (raw materials)

Photo angle

Schematic for a cosmetic powder and oil assembly cell

One operator performs steps 1-4. The second operator performs steps 5-8. A bottle is completed every 15 seconds. There are 8 bottles in process so stock-on-hand is 2 minutes.

108

◇ **Inspection (Quality Check)**
⊹ **Safety Check**
● **Stock-on-hand**

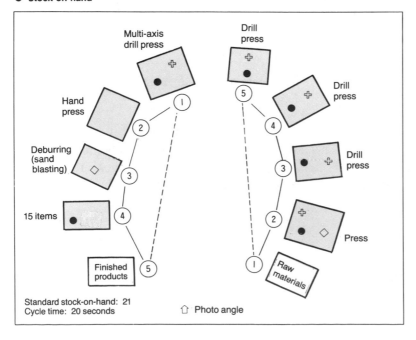

Multi-axis
drill press

Drill
press

Hand
press

Drill
press

Deburring
(sand
blasting)

Drill
press

15 items

Press

Finished
products

Raw
materials

Standard stock-on-hand: 21
Cycle time: 20 seconds

⇧ Photo angle

Standard operations in diecasting

- This is a U-shaped cell for machining and finishing diecastings.
- The cell has a visual control chart.
- A standard operations chart, a control chart, and a list of important QC points are visible in the cell.
- The standard sequence of operations is indicated by the lines in the schematic drawing. There are two workers in the cell.
- If the line looks disorganized, it is because they improve it daily.

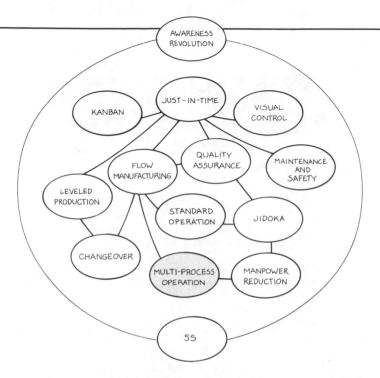

6. Multi-Process Handling

Multi-process handling means...

One operator handles several processes in a cell.

Points:

1. Clearly delineate the jobs performed by machine and the jobs performed by the operators. The machines can work independently (single-cycle automatics).
2. Make the cell U-shaped and give machines a *jidoka* function. After organizing the manufacturing system into cells, there may be some manufacturing processes which do not fit into cells. Put all these isolated island-type machine tools into one location and allocate operators to this area according to production quantities.
3. Operators should stand while working.
4. Train operators to be multi-skilled.

MACHINING PROCESSES

HORIZONTAL MULTI-MACHINE HANDLING
(ONE OPERATOR OPERATES MANY OF
THE SAME TYPE OF MACHINES)

PARTS A CELL

VERTICAL MULTI-PROCESS
HANDLING
(ONE OPERATOR RUNS
ALL THE MACHINES
IN A CELL. THE
MACHINES ARE
OF DIFFERENT
TYPES)

MILLING

LATHE

DEBURRING 2

DEBURRING 1

PROCESSED GOODS

UNPROCESSED GOODS

Multi-Machine Handling and Multi-Process Handling

Multi-machine handling

- An operator handles several machines with the same function.
- This is also called horizontal handling.
- This out-of-date method was part of the mass production system.

Machining process for automobile parts: This operator handles two machines —
in front of and behind him.

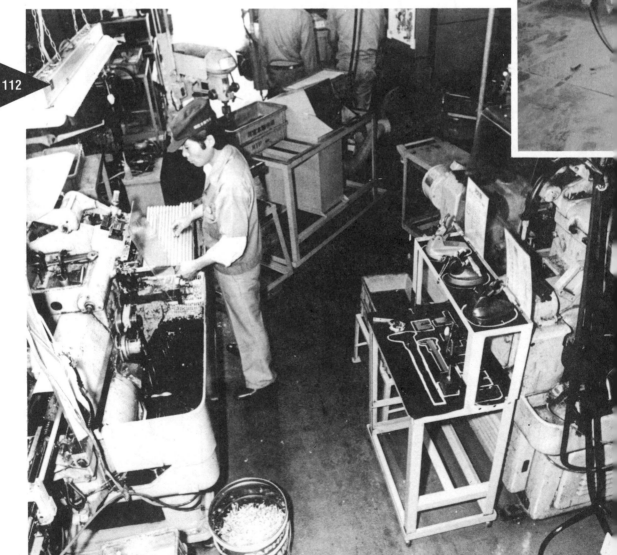

Multi-process handling for fabricating flooring materials: In this example of multi-process handling, workers developed a machine which reorients the material to be cut automatically. This process used to require two operators — now there is one.

Multi-process handling

- Multi-process handling means an operator handles more than one type of process, processing pieces one at a time depending on the production sequence.
- This is also called vertical handling.
- Multi-process handling is routinely used in manufacturing cells and is a basis of JIT production.

Multi-process handling in a machining process

- This is a machining cell for automotive parts.
- Here a numerical control (NC) machine and other machining processes have pulled together and adopted multi-process handling.
- During the NC process, the operator can handle additional processes.
- Because different processes are used in the cell depending on product type, machines are placed on casters for easy removal or reinsertion. Thus, the design of the cell is easily changed depending on the products being manufactured.
- This technique for cell formation is called the "key machine approach."

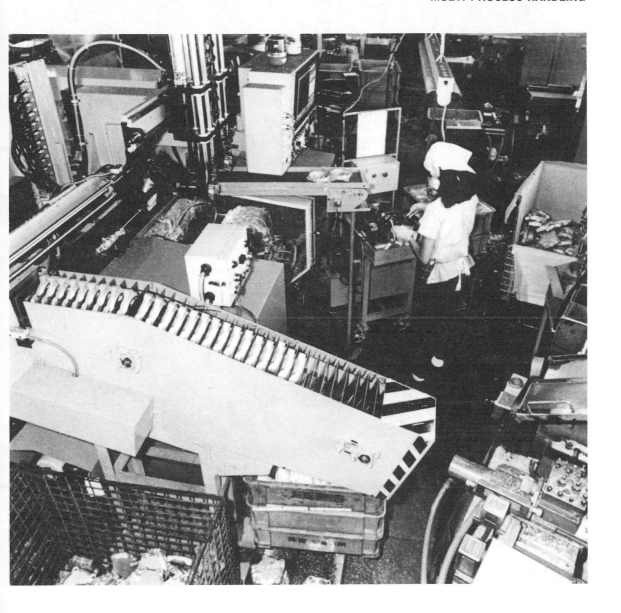

One unit of product shows us the required throughput time. The operator takes a door that has gone through the adhesive process to the drying area and puts it in the drying process. She removes a dry unit and takes it to the finishing process.

This is a woodworking line. Machining, drilling, and a few other jobs are performed here. Every machine has wheels for easy changeover of the cell. Depending on production quantities needed, one or two workers run the shop. That is, the output of the cell can be readily varied depending on the number of workers in the cell.

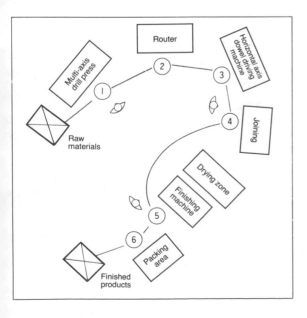

A woodworking assembly cell

- This is an assembly and packaging line for wooden doors.
- There is no in-process inventory within the cell.
- The workers perform multi-process handling.
- To reduce the number of operators, machines have been equipped with *jidoka* or automation with a human touch. The machines can complete the cycle initiated by the operators.
- Unlike the traditional batch system, doors are processed one at a time. This requires less space.

Casters

Machines bolted to the floor are permanently in place. Changes in the marketplace and plant improvements, however, may require changing machine layouts by product type. Floor bolts are our enemies! Machines must be movable. Casters will help.

Casters on a woodworking machine

- This is an example of casters used in the woodworking area.
- Operators usually stand when working.
- Efficiency is affected by raising the machine with casters. In this particular case, the height of the machine is unchanged.

An assembly line for audio equipment: This sound-proof room on casters gives the line the flexibility needed to adapt to changes of product movement. The movable room has two doors — on the left and right.

120

Casters

A movable hanger for automotive wire harnesses

- This movable hanger for automotive wire harnesses is now used between processes.
- Before, the hangers stood in one place.
- Workers had to remove the harnesses, roll them up, and transport them to the next process.
- The new method saves a lot of time!

This is a parts supply cart for VCR assembly. Before, ready-made carts were used to transport parts to the side of the line. These carts were also used to move empty boxes and did not remain at the line. As the quantity of parts needed increased, so did the clutter beside the line. Carts are now made in-house and remain at the line with the parts.

This is a grease table. Workers used to move the two- to five- meters-long harnesses to the table. The table now has been put on wheels and is moved to the harnesses.

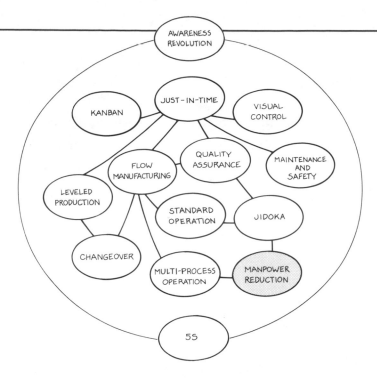

7. Reducing Worker Hours

Reducing worker hours means...

To produce goods with a minimum number of workers adjusting to changing market requirements.

Points:

1. Make equipment easy to move by attaching casters to machines.
2. Gather isolated machines into one location and institute multi-process handling. This is cell formation.
3. Standardize operations so everyone can perform the job.
4. Train operators through job rotation to be multi-skilled.
5. Don't assign a fixed number of workers to any process. It should vary by production quantity.

Reduction in Labor vs. Reduction in Workers

A comparison with conventional methods

- In the typical job shop manufacturing system, the company purchases a machine to improve efficiency.
- The machine is more automatic, so the operator needs more training but spends more time watching the machine work.
- The machine increases both facility and personnel costs.
- The machine only reduces the labor of the operator.
- This is what we call "reduction in labor."
- Reduction in labor only increases cost.

After pressing the start button on the NC machine, the operator simply watches. This is a waste.

Three-process handling for reduction in workers: After the NC machine was programmed and switched on, a strip of wood is attached to the edge of the board automatically. This allows the operator to handle two other operations.

Reduction in workers means producing goods with a minimum personnel cost.

A Cell

Reduction in workers in the diecast cell

- This is a diecasting cell that handles six processes.
- This is multi-process handling.
- Production capacity changes according to the number of operators.
- Machines have been modified to run without operators.
- When the machine is running, the operator can move to the next process. Machine and operator work separately.
- The line is U-shaped with the first process near the final one.
- Two or more operators work in a relay — passing the baton, so to speak, on to the next person.
- A single operator moves around the line processing one item at a time.

Passing the baton: In the U-shaped cell, the baton-passing zone must be wide enough to allow the first and second operators to perform the same job with the faster one helping the other.

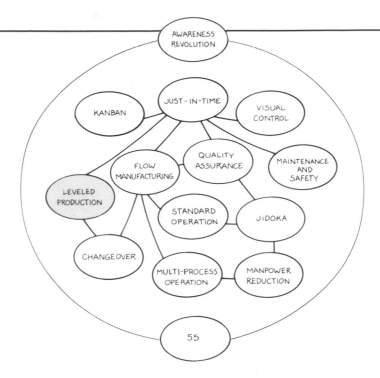

8. Leveling Production

Leveling production means...

To make the same quantity of an item every day.

Points:

1. Calculate cycle time based on monthly and daily production volumes.
2. Make a "cycle list" based on the cycle time. The cycle list details the order and number of the items being made on the line.
3. Shorten changeover times between the items.
4. Create a smooth flow.
5. Information and parts are delivered to the line several times daily. For the final assembly line, it means to level or smooth out the mix of the products being made. The idea is to make the same quantity of an item every day. The final assembly line can make a mix of products in any sequence, in any order.

MIXED MODEL FINAL ASSEMBLY

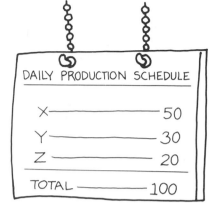

DAILY PRODUCTION SCHEDULE

X——————50
Y——————30
Z——————20
TOTAL————100

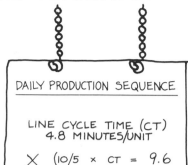

DAILY PRODUCTION SEQUENCE

LINE CYCLE TIME (CT)
4.8 MINUTES/UNIT

X (10/5 × CT = 9.6
Y (10/3 × CT = 16.0
Z (10/2 × CT = 24.0

LINE FLOW

PRODUCTION PROCEDURES
ARE REPEATED TEN TIMES

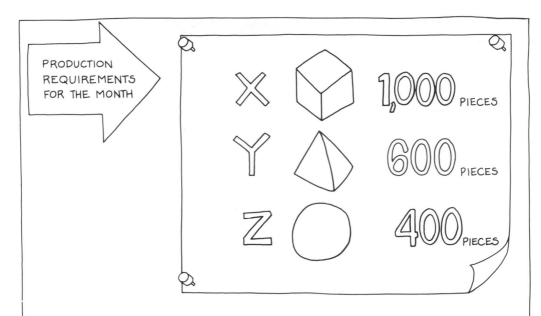

X	(cube)	1,000 PIECES
Y	(pyramid)	600 PIECES
Z	(sphere)	400 PIECES

HOW TO MAKE A PRODUCTION PLAN

1. MONTHLY

- A MONTHLY PLAN IS FOR PRODUCTS PRODUCED ON A MONTHLY SCHEDULE. AFTER 1000 X'S ARE MADE, SWITCH OVER TO Y, THEN TO Z.
- LINE EFFICIENCY, HOWEVER, DOES NOT ALWAYS RESULT IN PRODUCTION AND SALES EFFICIENCY.
- IF YOU PRODUCE ONLY ONE MODEL, THIS CAN WORK.
- FEW COMPANIES ONLY PRODUCE ONE PRODUCT. THIS METHOD IS OUT OF DATE.

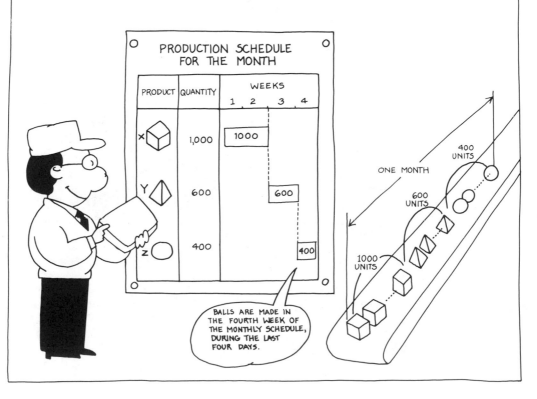

PRODUCTION SCHEDULE FOR THE MONTH

PRODUCT	QUANTITY	WEEKS 1	2	3	4
X	1,000	1000			
Y	600			600	
Z	400				400

BALLS ARE MADE IN THE FOURTH WEEK OF THE MONTHLY SCHEDULE, DURING THE LAST FOUR DAYS.

ONE MONTH

400 UNITS

600 UNITS

1000 UNITS

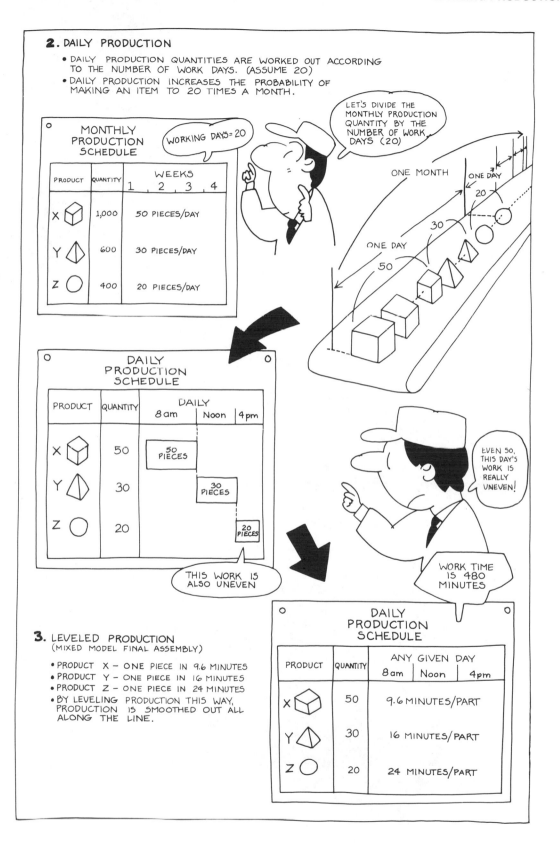

The sign says, "N17 finished products in under five steps."

Production leveling on a FAX assembly line

- This is an assembly line for FAX machines.
- After mechanical and electrical elements are assembled and inserted into the body, the FAX machines are moved to the final inspection area.
- Different FAX models with different specifications move along the same line.
- Numerous mechanical and electrical parts are needed all along the line.
- Mechanical and electrical subassembly lines are synchronized with the final line.
- The line is designed for multi-process handling and workers are trained to be multi-skilled.
- Rather than producing large quantities of one model, the mixed model line levels production by producing small quantities of various models.
- Parts subassembly lines, where products are assembled one at a time, are synchronized with the main line.

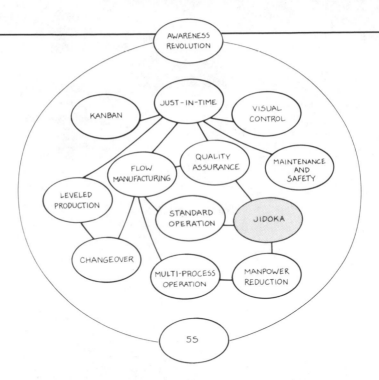

9. *Jidoka* (Automation with a Human Touch)

Automatic control of defects is autonomation . . .

To install a mechanism (sensor) in machines that permits them to detect defects and then a mechanism which stops the line or machine when defects occur. These machines add production value without the need of operators.

Points:

1. Machining operations should be performed by machines. Separate machines from operators.
2. An operator should not watch a machine capable of stopping itself when it produces a defect.
3. The concept of *jidoka*, begun in the machining division at Toyota Motor Company, can be applied to the assembly division.

Step 1. Manual:
Every operation is
done manually.
There is a dependence
on cheap labor.

**Step 2. Mech-
anization:** A
machine is used
for part of the
manual operation
making the job
easier but still
worker reliant.

136

Step 3. Automation:
Most operations are
automated with oper-
ators loading and
unloading the machines
and turning the
machines on to start
the automatic cycle.

Evolution toward Autonomation *(Jidoka)*

- There are many ways to machine the same item.
- Use simple tools and human labor alone.
- Machines work independently without human supervision.
- These are the processes in the evolution of autonomation.

Step 4. Automation with a human touch *(jidoka)*: This is an assembly line for electronics parts. One operator handles about ten machines. The operator loads the parts into the machine and starts the machining cycle. The machines automatically stop when the machining or processing cycle is completed. Some machines even unload the part themselves. This operator can perform his job while the machines do their jobs. These machines work independently of operators and have a zero-defect function.

Machine Independence

- Make it possible for a machine to run independently of the operator.
- This decouples the operator from the machine.

Jidoka of a small washing machine: You've seen this machine in the flow manufacturing photographs. This machine is equipped to automatically eject a defective part. The operator loads the machine and initiates the processing cycle. The machine does everything else independent of operators.

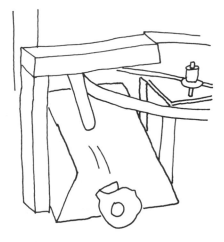

138

Harness-measuring equipment

- This machine measures out harness material and rolls it up on a drum.
- A metal sensor is located under the drum.
- Harnesses used to be purchased from a subcontractor who measured and cut the harnesses to length.
- Inventory piled up because production quantities changed frequently.
- An operator now loads harness material on the drum and turns the switch on.
- The machine automatically measures, cuts to proper length, and rolls up the harness.
- The operator meanwhile does something else while the machine is working.

140

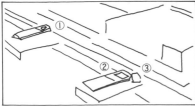

1. Video ON
2. Power ON
3. Sensor

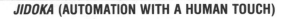
A Zero-Defect Operation

- A machine that is only automated can produce defects.
- We need a machine that never produces defects even without an operator.
- This means we must make machines think — not just move and perform work.

Jidoka of a VCR assembly line

- This line inspects VCR machines.
- Inspectors used to turn on the power and video switches.
- This required two inspectors and two sets of inspection equipment.
- Method improvements now require only one set of equipment.
- The right sensor turns on the power while the left sensor turns on the video.
- An inspector can now check quality while walking along the assembly line.

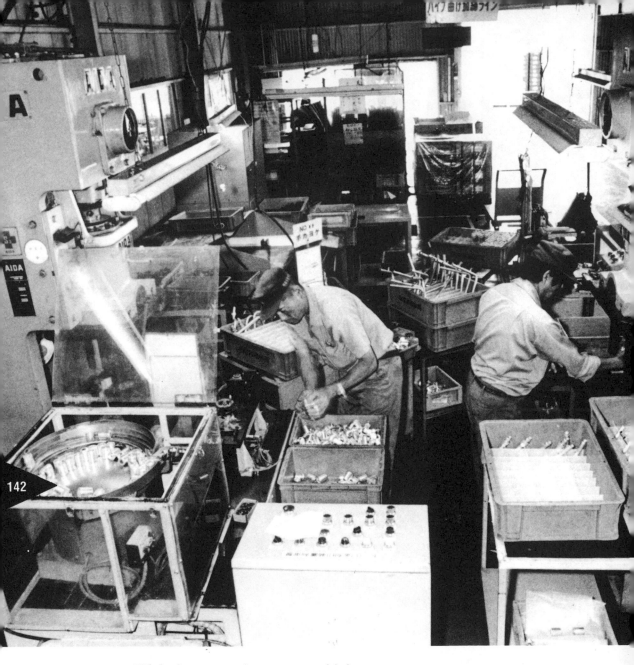

Jidoka in automotive parts machining

- This worker is bending automotive parts.
- There are many similar parts on the line.
- If hc chooses the wrong part by mistake, a defective product is produced down the line.
- This machine, however, has a *poka-yoke* function — it does not start if the wrong part is inserted.

Jidoka of a small caulking machine: This shows the automation of a machine used to caulk electronic parts. It is an example of putting a caulking machine on the line in flow manufacturing. The caulking machine is used for one-piece production and permits parallel processing of human and machine work.

A machine with a *poka-yoke* function.

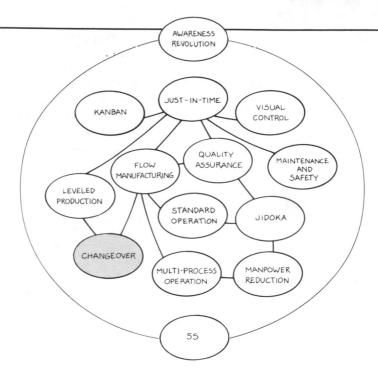

10. Changeover

Changeover means...

Changing dies, cutting tools, workholders, or operation methods according to changes in specifications. We call a line or cell that can make these changes quickly "flexible and robust."

Points:

1. Changeover time is the time that lapses between the last finished product of one type and the first good product of another type or model.
2. Changeover time is the sum of internal and external changeover times.
3. External time refers to the changeover (setup) time spent while the process is running.
4. If the process must be stopped to perform the changeover task, this is internal time.
5. It's important to convert internal into external changeovers.
6. Remember that bolts are our enemies! Also, move the hands — but never the feet or base of the machine or tool.
7. Implementing the 5S's is essential.

Changeover Procedures

External vs. internal changeover: Internal changeovers are conducted while machine is stopped. External changeovers are conducted while machine is running. Use external changeover.

Analyze the entire changeover operation and sort out what are internal operations, external operations, and wasted motions.

**Procedure #2:
Identify and
eliminate waste.**

**Procedure #3:
Make internal
changeovers
external.**

**Procedure #1:
Analyze changeover.**

**Procedure #4:
Improve internal
changeover.**

**Procedure #5:
Improve external
changeover.**

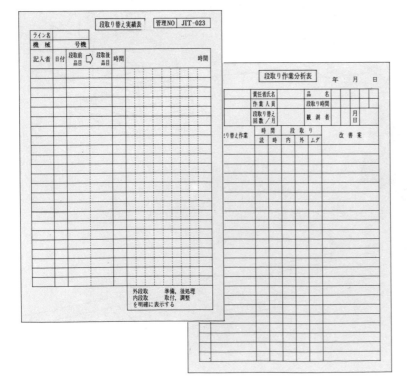

段取り替え実績表　　管理NO　JIT-023

ライン名
機　械　　号機
記入者　日付　段取前　段取後　時間　　　　　　時間
　　　　　　品目　　品目

外段取　準備、後処理
内段取　取付、調整
を明確に表示する

段取り作業分析表　　年　月　日

責任者氏名　　品　名
作業人員　　段取り時間
段取り替え　観測者　月
回数／月　　　　　日
り替え作業　時間　段取り　改善案
　　　　読　時　内　外　ムダ

Eliminate the waste of searching: Keep tools and jigs in their proper places.

Eliminating waste in internal changeover:

1. Eliminate bolts entirely or, if they are still needed, make them tighten with one turn.
2. Make all dies the same size on the outside although they differ inside — just like a cassette for a tape deck.
3. Eliminate adjustments.
4. Convert in-line changeovers to parallel changeovers.

Eliminating waste in external changeover:

1. Proper arrangement *(seiri)* and orderliness *(seiton)*.
2. Use carts exclusively for this operation.
3. Assign workers for changeover.

Changeover in Wire Harness Inspection

- The inspection process for wire harnesses uses electrical inspection boards. For each type of harness, there is a different board.
- The inspection boards used to be located elsewhere.
- So at every changeover, someone had to retrieve the new inspection boards and bring them to the manufacturing area.
- All the inspection boards are now placed next to the inspection process.
- This shortened changeover time.

Setup time in the lead cutter: This photograph shows the jig that holds the leads for the wire harnesses. The leads are cut to lengths in this jig. Butterfly-shaped bolts have replaced standard hexagonal bolts. This has shortened changeover time.

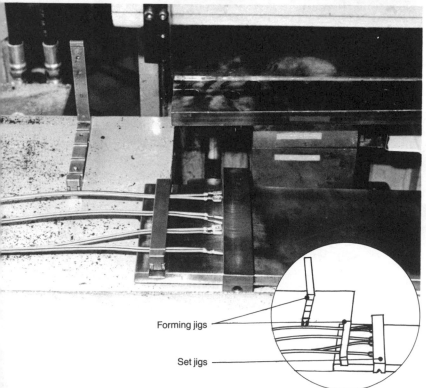

Forming jigs

Set jigs

External changeover in forming wire harnesses: This process molds rubber onto a wire harness. Harnesses used to be loaded directly into the dies. It took 10 seconds to load the harness and the operators were idle while the machine was processing 2 sets of the 4 parts. To improve this operation, forming jigs were prepared, each holding 4 parts. While the 4 parts are being molded, the next 4 harnesses are loaded into the second die, eliminating waiting time for the operator. Harnesses are delivered to the process in sets of 4, further shortening the loading time for harnesses in the dies.

Changeover on a wooden cabinet assembly line

- This is an assembly line for wooden kitchen cabinets.
- Workers here are attaching doors to cabinets.
- Cabinets come in different styles and colors.
- Doors come in five patterns and three different colors.
- Doors are assembled elsewhere in the plant on another separate line in sequence with the cabinets. Doors are transported to the line on carts.
- Smooth assembly requires rapid changeover from one cabinet style to the next.
- Hinges are attached to the doors prior to assembly according to tags attached to the doors. The doors are then installed on the correct cabinets.

Preparing doors for wooden cabinets: This is the process where doors are prepared for their respective cabinets. This worker transports the doors from the parts warehouse according to a computer printout and places them on carts in their production sequence. Tearing off part of the list with the product's name, she attaches it to the door. In the next process, doors are drilled using automatic machines, which means the worker performs external changeovers with the machine running.

Die change in a press shop for stainless steel sinks.

- This is a press shop for stainless sinks.
- The die for this 1,200-ton press weighs 7.5 tons.
- Previously, forklifts were used once a day to change dies. Lot sizes were very large.
- Lots are smaller now and the number of product types has increased, requiring three or four die changes a day.
- Workers have adopted a quick die change system that has reduced changeover time from 80 minutes to 40 minutes.
- Workers now perform more external changeover operations
- The workforce has decreased from five to two operators. There are also fewer mistakes made during changeover.
- They are now trying to reduce setup times to under 10 minutes. This is the SMED (single-minute exchange of die) system of Shigeo Shingo.

Improving external operations can shorten changeover times dramatically.

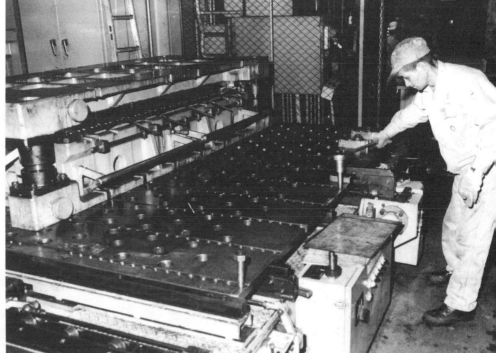

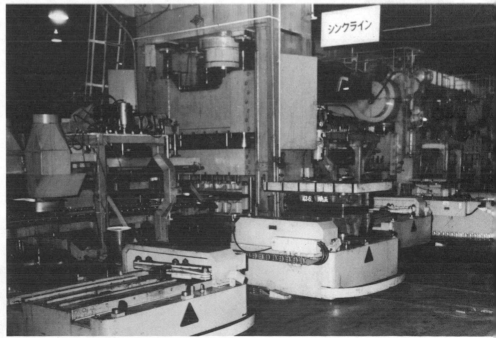

Quick die changes are performed on these presses, which are arranged in a flow manufacturing system.

Changing cutters on a horizontal milling machine

Operators developed a method to change cutting tools without removing the brackets by drilling holes in the sides of the brackets. The next cutter is prepared externally. Special tools and carts were made for this operation, reducing changeover time from 1 hour to 6 minutes.

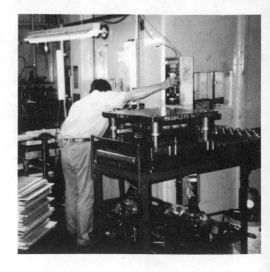

Cutting tools for the machining center

Cutting tools for the machining center are preset externally and placed on a cart making them portable and accessible during changeover.

Double-headed milling machine

Jigs once stored on racks are now kept on carts of the same height as the table of the milling machine, allowing quick and easy changeovers. Setup time has been reduced from 30 minutes to 5 minutes.

156

A numerically controlled (NC) lathe

Changeover time for jaws of this 3-jaw chuck has been reduced from 50 minutes to 3 minutes.

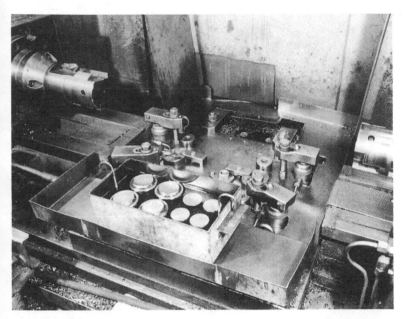

Double-headed drill press

Once the jig has been placed on the machine's table, don't move the jig's base. Keep the jig base the same and modify it for different parts using adaptors. One-touch changeover is now possible. Machine stoppage for changeover for this process has been cut from 7 hours to 6 minutes.

Multiple spindle drill press

The jig in this multiple spindle drill press is designed to hold 2 parts. Drill bushings (to locate the drills) are put on both sides of the vertical plate, which maintains accuracy and reduces changeover time from 60 minutes to 5 minutes.

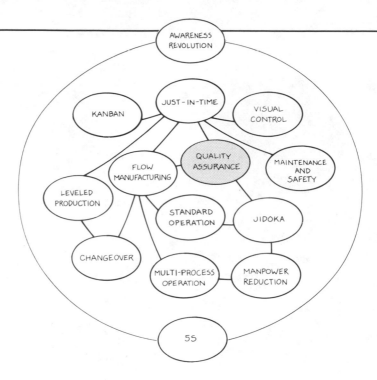

11. Quality Assurance

Quality assurance means...

Maintaining quality using workers, manufacturing system design, and production methods to satisfy customer needs.

Points:

1. When a defect is discovered, immediately find the cause and correct it.
2. Eliminate wastes arising from unnecessary transporting, waiting, and delay by smoothing the flow of the materials in the manufacturing system.
3. Make a chart of current standard operations.
4. Produce by the piece — not by lot. Automate the line to never produce defects.
5. Develop *poka-yoke* (defect prevention) devices to prevent defects from being manufactured by the process.

Starting and Maintaining a Companywide Defect Prevention *(Poka-yoke)* Program

Operators are good at producing defects.

- They think they're working correctly.
- But defects occur and they don't even realize it.

Users are good at finding defects.

- They don't buy a product to find defects.
- When they find defects, they can't use the product.

To have zero defects, a users' viewpoint must be adopted throughout the production process.

Zero Defects Checklist						Name:					Date:
Job	Methods	Standards	Inspections	Defects	Causes of defects	Three current status points	Three counter-action points	Evaluation of counter-measures	Implemen-tation time	Supervisor

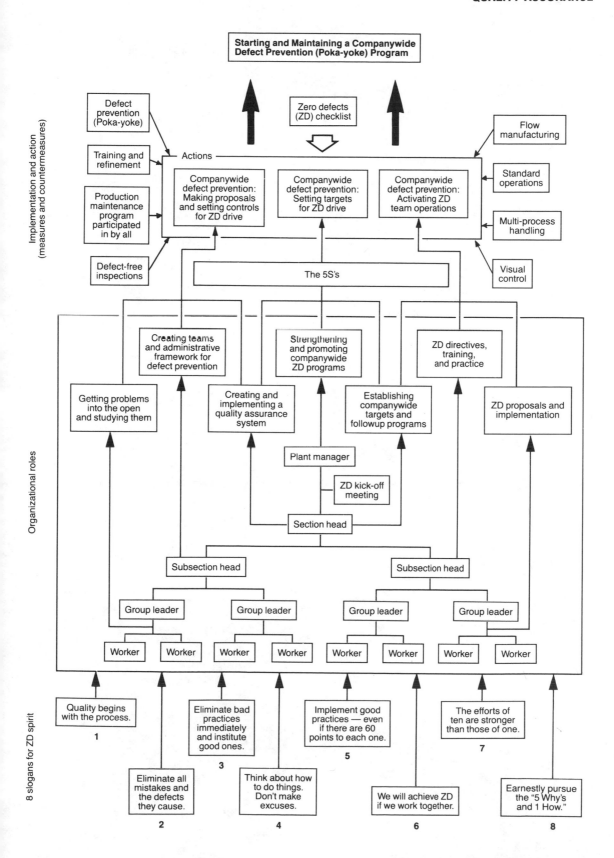

Starting and Maintaining a Companywide Defect Prevention (Poka-yoke) Program

Zero defects (ZD) checklist

Implementation and action (measures and countermeasures)

Defect prevention (Poka-yoke)

Training and refinement

Production maintenance program participated in by all

Defect-free inspections

Actions

Flow manufacturing

Standard operations

Multi-process handling

Visual control

Companywide defect prevention: Making proposals and setting controls for ZD drive

Companywide defect prevention: Setting targets for ZD drive

Companywide defect prevention: Activating ZD team operations

The 5S's

Organizational roles

Creating teams and administrative framework for defect prevention

Strengthening and promoting companywide ZD programs

ZD directives, training, and practice

Getting problems into the open and studying them

Creating and implementing a quality assurance system

Establishing companywide targets and followup programs

ZD proposals and implementation

Plant manager

ZD kick-off meeting

Section head

Subsection head

Subsection head

Group leader

Group leader

Group leader

Group leader

Worker Worker Worker Worker Worker Worker Worker Worker

8 slogans for ZD spirit

Quality begins with the process.
1

Eliminate all mistakes and the defects they cause.
2

Eliminate bad practices immediately and institute good ones.
3

Think about how to do things. Don't make excuses.
4

Implement good practices — even if there are 60 points to each one.
5

We will achieve ZD if we work together.
6

The efforts of ten are stronger than those of one.
7

Earnestly pursue the "5 Why's and 1 How."
8

Quality inspection of VCRs

- This photograph portrays quality inspection of VCRs.
- Every product is inspected.
- Therefore, efficient and economical inspection methods are needed.
- Operations have been improved with automatic on-and-off switches and visual inspection in a chair-free assembly process.

This sensor is used to turn on an electric switch.

Quality inspection of telephone equipment

- Here we see an inspection process for telephone equipment.
- Every product is inspected.
- Inspection is synchronized with the assembly line and products flow by one by one.
- Inspectors report defects at once to the assembly line.
- Problems are solved quickly, thus preventing defects from multiplying.
- They are next going to eliminate chairs and make their line flexible enough to meet changes in production quantities.

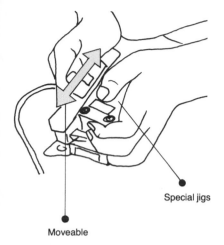

Special jigs

Moveable

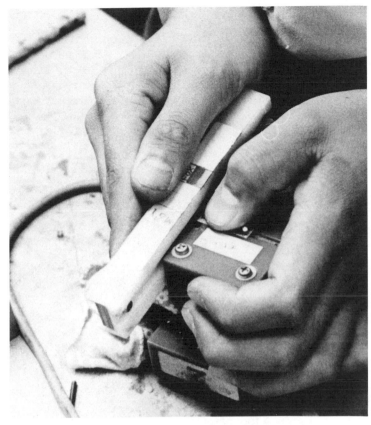

The sensitivity and edges of a sensor are being inspected here. Workers made a special tool to check all products in a short time. This inspection process runs parallel to the UV coating process (10 to 15 seconds) and enables inspection to be done while UV coating is being applied.

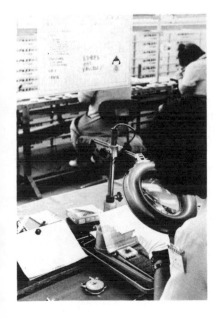

In this workplace, quality inspection of electronic parts occurs along the assembly line. It's important to identify defects and take quick action.

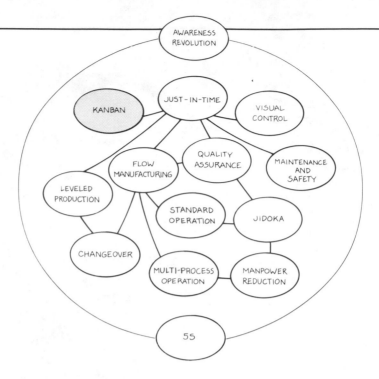

12. *Kanban*

Kanban are...

A tool of the just-in-time system that carries information for production control. They are frequently tags or pieces of paper.

Rules for the use of *kanban*:

1. The subsequent process goes to the former process to get parts.
2. The former process produces the quantity removed (pulled) by the subsequent process.
3. Quality is built into the product. Defects are never sent to the subsequent process.
4. *Kanban* always accompany products on the line thus ensuring thorough visual control.
5. Production quantities are leveled to avoid fluctuations and eliminate wastes.
6. Reducing the number of *kanban* increases their sensitivity and reveals places where process improvements are needed. This is inventory control.

Using *Kanban* as a Work Order

- There are two ways to use *kanban*:
  1. Production Ordering (POK)
  2. For withdrawal or conveyance (WLK)
- POKs are work orders that include some operation instructions.
- The examples on these pages are from a woodworking plant.
- The front of the *kanban* gives operation information and the back gives specifications.

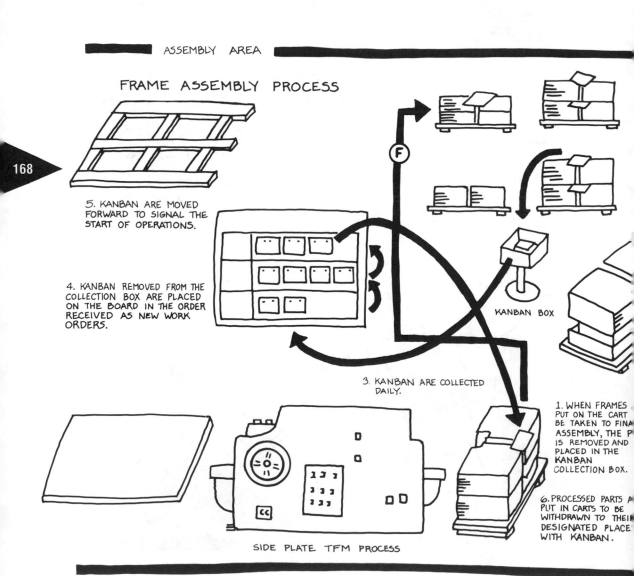

ASSEMBLY AREA

FRAME ASSEMBLY PROCESS

5. KANBAN ARE MOVED FORWARD TO SIGNAL THE START OF OPERATIONS.

4. KANBAN REMOVED FROM THE COLLECTION BOX ARE PLACED ON THE BOARD IN THE ORDER RECEIVED AS NEW WORK ORDERS.

KANBAN BOX

3. KANBAN ARE COLLECTED DAILY.

1. WHEN FRAMES PUT ON THE CART BE TAKEN TO FINA ASSEMBLY, THE P IS REMOVED AND PLACED IN THE KANBAN COLLECTION BOX.

6. PROCESSED PARTS A PUT IN CARTS TO BE WITHDRAWN TO THEI DESIGNATED PLACE WITH KANBAN.

SIDE PLATE TFM PROCESS

NAME OF FRAME		QUANTITY
SIDE PLATE FRAME Y828		30

CATEGORY	DIMENSIONS	REQUIRED QUANTITY
VERTICAL CORE	11.9 × 90 × 1830	60
VERTICAL CORE	11.9 × 165 × 1830	30
HORIZONTAL CORE	11.9 × 40 × 389.5	300
HORIZONTAL CORE	11.9 × 50 × 389.5	60
HORIZONTAL CORE	11.9 × 75 × 389.5	60

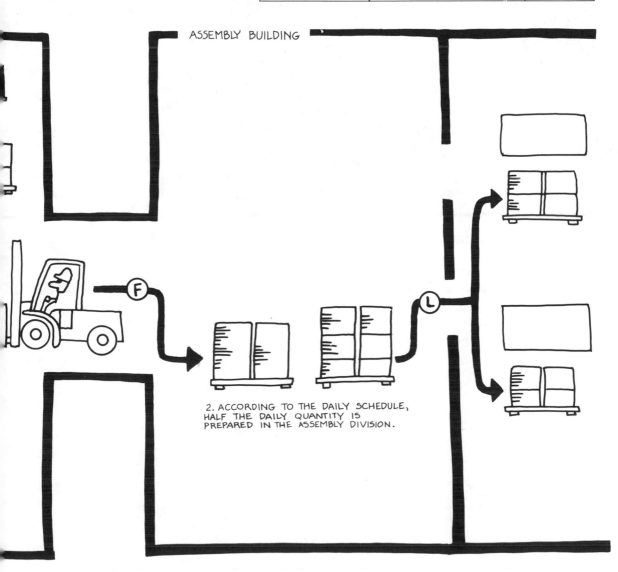

ASSEMBLY BUILDING

2. ACCORDING TO THE DAILY SCHEDULE, HALF THE DAILY QUANTITY IS PREPARED IN THE ASSEMBLY DIVISION.

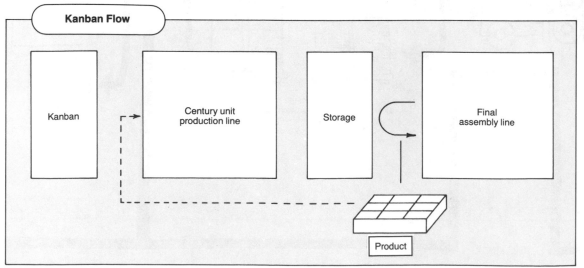

Kanban Flow

| Kanban | Century unit production line | Storage | Final assembly line |

Product

Kanban as a production order

- This is a container for sensor units.
- *Kanban* are used as work orders providing operational instruction with the line or cell.
- At the final assembly line, harnesses are installed into sensors.
- The POK is removed from the container.
- When a *kanban* returns to the area where sensor units are built, production begins.
- POKs contain the necessary information on specifications.

A,B,C down and
1,2,3 across.

Kanban in a woodworking plant

- *Kanban* are used to control supplier deliveries. Invoices are stored in this large rack.
- Invoices are sorted by computer.
- *Kanban* move along with parts and are exchanged for invoices when the parts are needed. It is easy to see what is in the rack.
- This is a good example of *kanban* as a work order.
- This is a good example of *kanban* as a work order with visual control.
- It's taken a lot of effort to reach this stage!

These *kanban* cards give codes for name, part number, operator, and supervisor. The PO2 card, for instance, refers to the side plate TFM process.

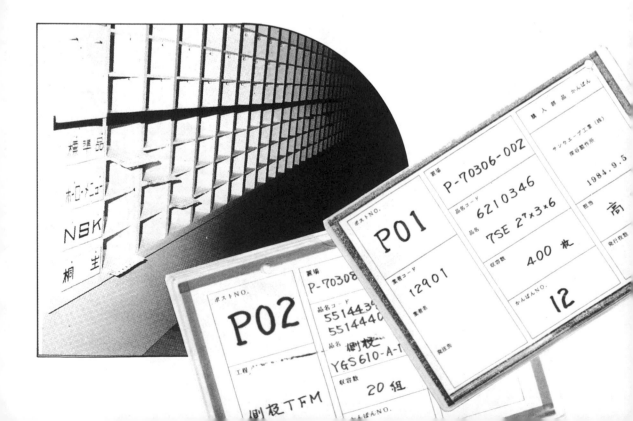

Withdrawal *kanban* for telephone equipment assembly line

- This photograph shows an area from an assembly line for telephone equipment.
- Different types of equipment are assembled on this line.
- Subassemblies for the equipment are supplied using *kanban*.
- This partitioned box is a *kanban* used to transport a subassembly — a printed circuit board with connector — from the subassembly area to the final assembly line.
- Specifications are written on the side of the box (type, quantity, destination, etc.).
- The withdrawal *kanban* connect the subassembly area with the final assembly line for telephone equipment.

Components for harness assembly are hung on hanger *kanban*. When the hangers are empty, they are returned to the harness manufacturing area where the needed quantity is made and placed again on the hangers. They then are transported to the assembly area.

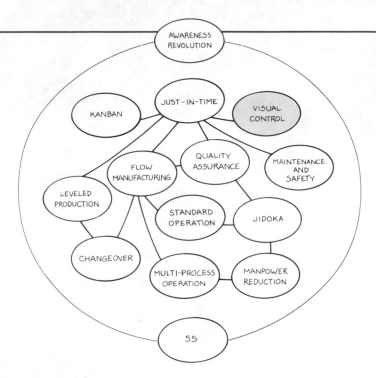

13. Visual Control

Visual control means...

Making it possible for everyone to see whether the situation is right or wrong and wherein lies the waste.

Points:

1. For visual control, red lights and signboards are used.
2. *Andon* (line-stop alarm lights) are used to inform people on the floor of problems, parts supply, and exchange of cutting tools.
3. The production control board is used to inform people of the production rate of the line or reasons for a line stop.
4. *Kanban* are tools used to prevent overproduction.
5. Defective parts or products are displayed in the factory.

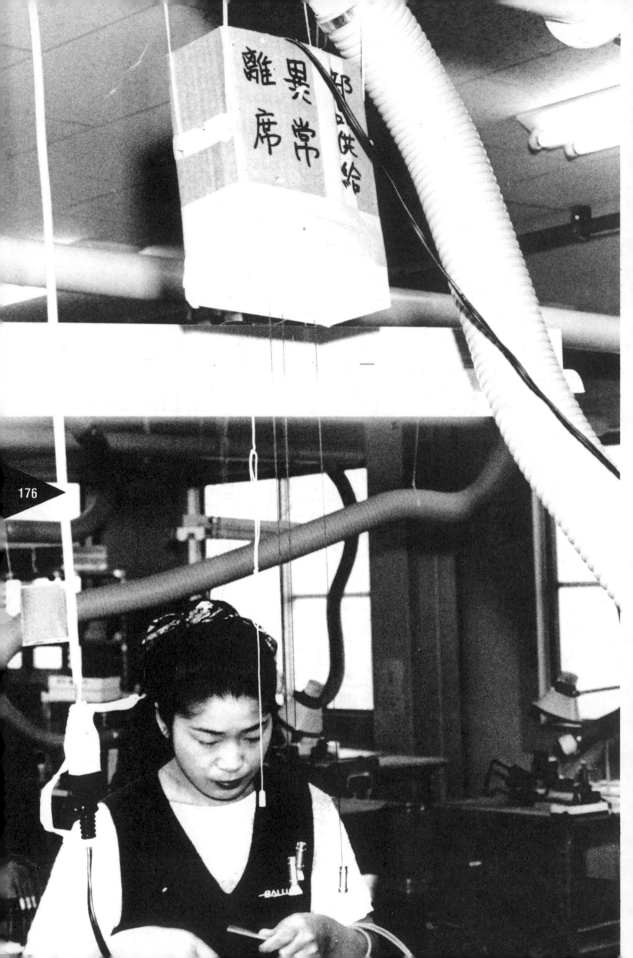

Andon (Line-Stop Alarm Light)

Andon for sensor assembly line

- *Andon* tells you of a problem in the line such as abnormal conditions, parts shortages, or defective products.
- In this photograph, an *andon* is used for sensor assembly.
- This is a flow production line.
- There are usually three workers here.
- Workers turn on the *andon* when they discover a problem, a parts shortage, or when they leave the work site.
- When the *andon* light comes on, a buzzer goes off.
- Line foremen must correct the situation as quickly as possible.

Andon

It is important to establish a system where managers and supervisors can see at a glance that something is happening on the factory floor.

Andon in a VCR line: The switch is located by this operator. When she flips the switch, a buzzer goes off and the light above her head comes on as well as larger overhead lights along the line. Workers at first hesitated to press the switch but now do so whenever they find a problem.

Signboards

Improvement board in an electronics equipment factory

- When improvement activity is carried on successfully, the design of the workplace changes daily.
- Once conditions are improved, it's difficult to remember how it was before the improvement.
- In factories that have undergone a lot of improvement, operators themselves can't believe what they used to do.
- Looking at the "before" and "after" photographs, we wonder if we really worked that way.
- Improvements must be kept track of . . .
- Otherwise we'll never remember how much we've improved.
- Letting everyone know how we've improved can be a motivation tool for the next improvement.
- One improvement triggers the next.
- Therefore it's important to let everyone know even the smallest improvement.

Improvement

Before Improvement

After Improvement

Effect: The distance between Process 1 and 2 was shortened from 6 meters to 0.5 meter. The number of operators was reduced from three to two.

Expenses: ¥ 149,000 ($1,192 U.S.) was spent for cylinders and boosters.

Improvement: Process 1 is moved closer to Process 2. We built a new machine and modified the other. We moved the air drying tank to eliminate transporting waste. We reduced work-in-process inventories because there is really no space for any.

Improvement items list				Control supervisor	
No.	Date	Problem	Implementation date	Implementor	Remarks

Signboards

Posted (or standing) *kanban*

- This is the improvement board in an electronics equipment assembly factory.
- 5S activity is happening companywide.
- Then managers visit the plant and point out problem areas, photographs are taken.
- The photographs are then pinned to the board with time estimates for improvement.
- The division manager reviews the improvement and writes "ok" if it is accepted.
- This factory's division managers visit the line several times a day.

This is the "5S Public Relations Board" of an electronics equipment maker. It's located where everyone can see it. It may be the angle of the photograph, but it could be mounted a little higher.

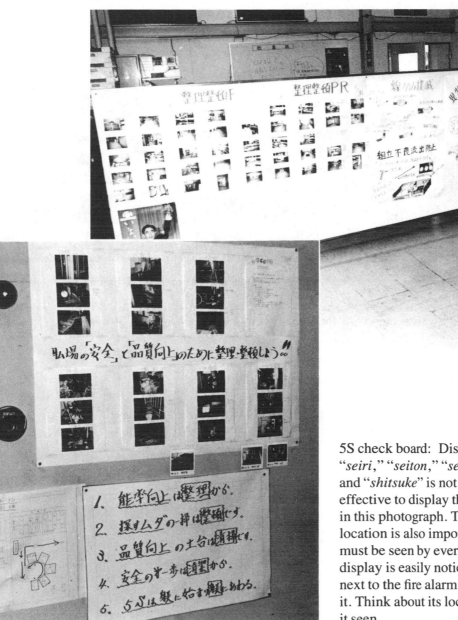

5S check board: Displaying the words "*seiri*," "*seiton*," "*seiketsu*," "*seiso*," and "*shitsuke*" is not enough. It's more effective to display the results as shown in this photograph. The signboard's location is also important because it must be seen by everyone. This 5S display is easily noticed because it is next to the fire alarm. Don't just display it. Think about its location and make it seen.

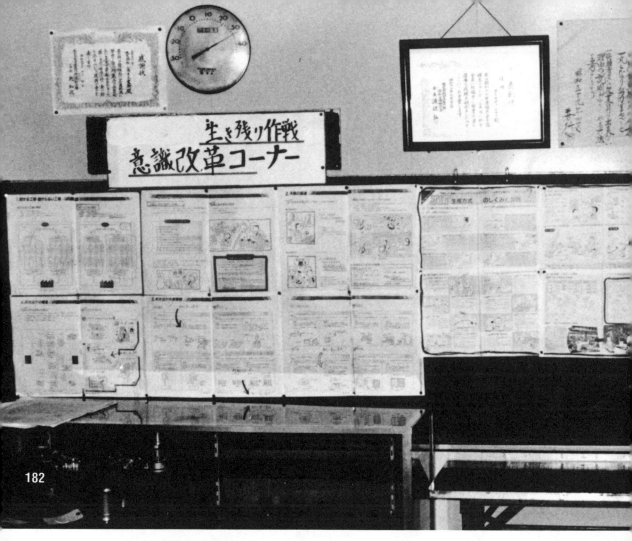

Signboards

An "awareness revolution" board

- Factories have areas other than work areas.
- There might be a smoking area or a rest area.
- This factory has an "awareness revolution" area.
- Do you have anything like this?
- For a company to survive, everyone's awareness must change.
- There will be no changes without this.

A display of defective products: Defects not only increase costs but damage a company's credibility. Business is based on trust and defects should never occur. The first thing to do is change the awareness of workers. Make a list of defects and post it. If this is not effective enough, display the actual defectives. This photograph shows such a display in a factory. We can tell which line produced the defective parts.

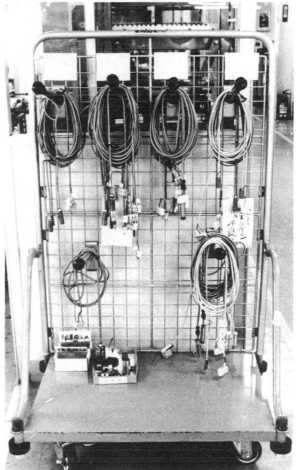

184

Signboards

Signs that show processes

- This is a cosmetics assembly line.
- Certain processes change location along the line when different products are being assembled.
- Each process in this factory has its own sign hung above it.

Water beetle

Water beetles walk in circles on the water easily and swiftly. Any factory producing various products requires people to transport parts and materials from the manufacturing cells to the line several times daily. These people are like water beetles (and the factory floor is water) traveling the kanban loops time after time.

This is a VCR assembly line. Parts are supplied to it several times daily. No inventory is placed beside the line unless it is within an operator's reach. The "water beetle" moves around supplying parts. To make it easier for this person to find the correct locations, each process has a sign.

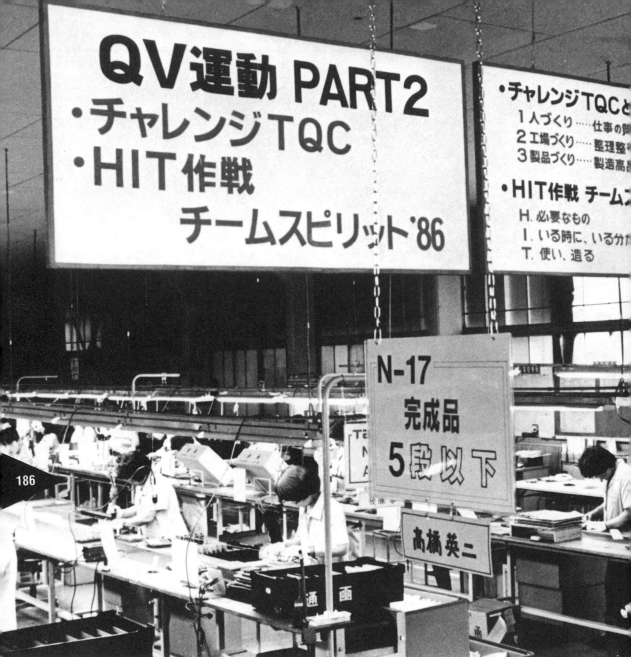

Signboards

Signs to express goals

- "Be united!" This is important for any factory.
- A slogan is needed to get everyone moving toward the same goal.
- It must be understood by everybody.
- "Team spirit!" may sound like the military — but it's needed to achieve goals.

Visual control chart: Because company-wide activities aim at employees, slogans tend to be placed in the cafeteria. It is also effective, however, to show your suppliers or affiliated companies what you are doing. This improves the relationship. In this company, policy statements are posted on the wall above the communication boxes with suppliers. This is a good idea.

Slogans easily seen by all workers.

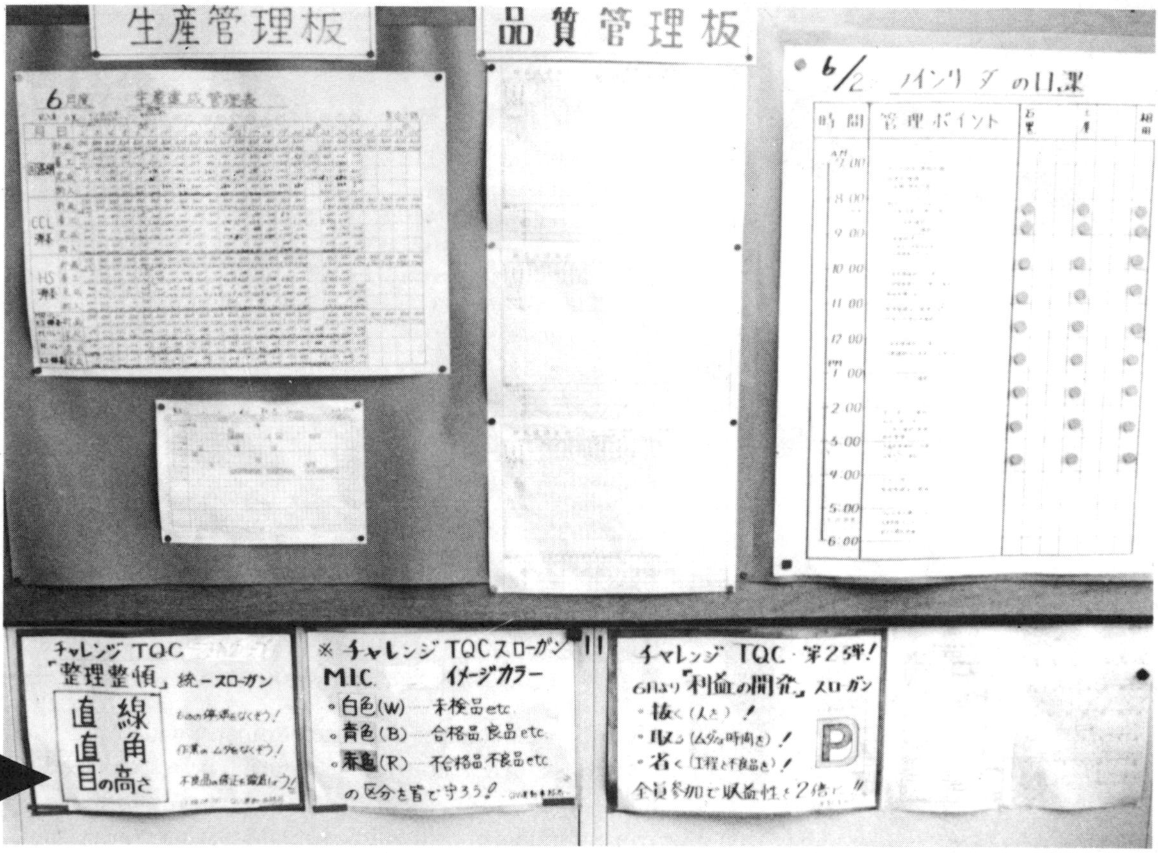

生産管理板　　品質管理板

188

Signboards

A scheduling control chart

- Proper arrangement *(seiri)* and orderliness *(seiton)* are easier said than done.
- Because it is difficult to specify methods down to the smallest detail, we might think it unnecessary to explain such details.
- But in companies like that, 5S signs are meaningless.
- For example, if we indicate exact locations for things but we don't keep them there, what good is it?
- 5S slogans show our willingness to keep the rules once they are established.

One group's work scheduling chart.

Operation control chart: This chart clearly shows us what has to be done.

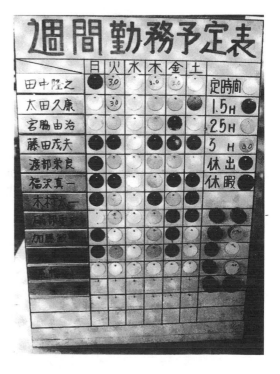

Signboards

Production control board

- This is not just another bulletin board.
- A listing of "Improvement Principles" is right in the center.
- We can see how vigorously they emphasize improvement.
- Even the ashtray is clean.
- The fifth of the 5S's — discipline — has been implemented here.

月 日~日	生産管理板	ライン名			サイクルタイム	
		工程名				
		作業内容			標準作業人員	
		前工程		後工程	記入者	

時間	標準数 累計	( ) 実績数/累計	理由	( ) 実績数/累計	理由	( ) 実績数/累計	理由	( ) 実績数/累計	理由	( ) 実績数/累計	理由	( ) 実績数/累計	理由	( )・( ) 実績数/累計	理由	( ) 実績数/累計	理由	( ) 実績数/累計	理由
実績																			
累計実績	累計差異																		
異常処置																			

Production control chart: We often see production control charts showing daily production volumes. In this factory, however, volumes for ten days at a time are shown so everyone can witness the changes. In many factories, some workers do the same job every day regardless of quantity changes. What we need today is the flexibility to change operations according to production requirements (customer demand).

Improvement principles: This photograph was taken at a medical equipment manufacturer's plant. It has been a few months since they started their improvement activity. Beginning with the 5S's, they eliminated ten worktables and shelves and removed the chairs. Changes are visible everywhere. The slogan on the wall lists the rules.

時間	数量
AM 10:00	19
12:15	42
PM 3:00	64
5:15	87

Signboards

Production control board

- We often hear the words "information strategy" or "real time communication."
- Computers are now commonly used in production facilities and we now find terminals and screens on the factory floor.
- Computers process information quickly.
- This is because everything in the job shop is *RUSH*!
- But we can process information quickly without spending money on computers.
- *Kanban* can be used to communicate the actual quantities being built against the hourly target quantities.

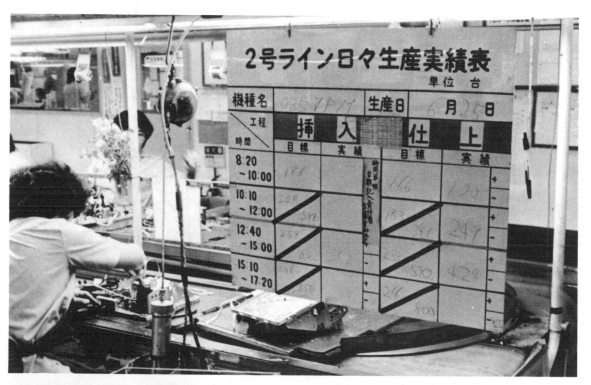

Hourly production chart: This is a conveyor line for assembling baseboard in an electronics equipment manufacturer. On the left is a signboard showing the hourly records of the actual production volume every day. Above is another chart showing the beginning and finished production quantities indicated side by side. June 25 shows them being a little behind.

Digital production control

Signboards

Materials warehouse map

- This is the materials storage area of an electronics equipment maker.
- Assign parts addresses to the shelves and then make a map like this one.
- Imitate a municipal or neighborhood map — it's very similar!
- Don't make it too detailed.
- Make it easy to understand.
- Use colors.
- Make it so easy to follow that even the company president could find something if asked to transport a part.

Here, the addressed locations of parts are displayed on racks in accordance with the layout (the map) of the warehouse. Because there are numerous small parts, transport workers would be in big trouble if parts weren't stored properly — especially during design changes. Looking at this example we understand the importance of orderliness and proper storage in the 5S's.

Addresses

- They show location. We receive mail because there is an address.
- They are composed of street name and number. Different parts should never share the same address.

Visual control on the parts shelves: Each shelf has an assigned number with the location of parts clearly indicated.

Signboards

A visual locker

- Indicating location is one of the 5S methods of proper arrangement *(seiton)*.
- This means assigning addresses in the factory.
- It sounds simple but it's not easy.
- It's difficult to understand even if addresses are assigned.
- So, if you do it, do it effectively.
- Make it easily seen by everyone.
- The photograph is black and white — but the signboard is really vividly painted.
- How do you like it?

A factory's face is its entrance. If our faces are dirty, business will flee. Yet we often see empty and half-empty noodle bowls stacked at factory entrances waiting for the noodle restaurant's delivery man to retrieve them. Would you do business with a company like that? Of course not. Products reflect the attitude of the workers. Clean, self-disciplined factories produce fewer defects.

The sign in this photo says: "Thanks for your day's work! Let's keep the effort going, now and in the future."

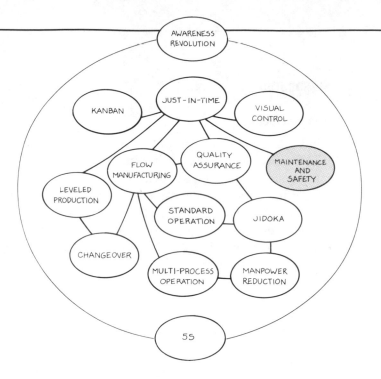

14. Maintenance and Safety

Maintenance and safety means...

Preventing equipment and facilities from breaking down. This increases a factory's productivity. Safety's role is to prevent accidents by setting rules to follow.

Points:

Make these three rules of maintenance a habit:

1. Cleanup
2. Oil application
3. Check

Follow these four safety rules:

1. Separate machines from operators.
2. Follow safety standards to the letter.
3. Follow rules.
4. Find the real causes of problems and prevent them from recurring.

Maintenance

- Machines used for JIT should be small, dedicated, and slow.
- They are not expensive to install.
- Mobility is more important than a machine's production rate.
- This means machine maintenance is essential.

Company-wide maintenance activity: This photograph is from a semiconductor manufacturer. Each team reports its activities and results. This can motivate people to be more conscious about maintenance.

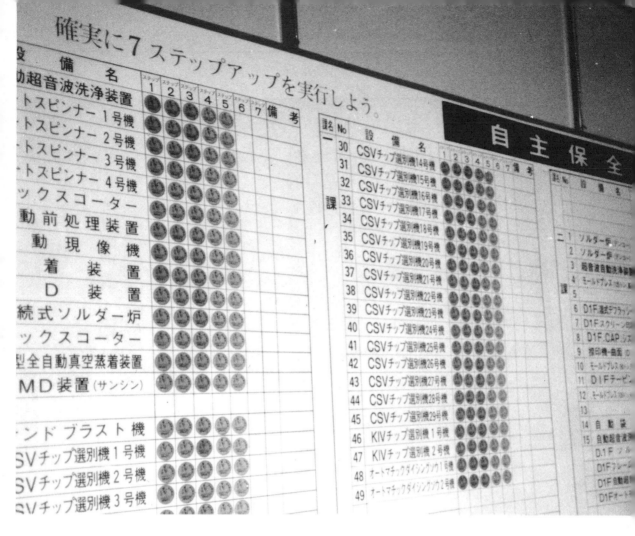

確実に7ステップアップを実行しよう。

自 主 保 全

The sign above says, "Let's improve progress in voluntary maintenance activity!"

The Winning TPM Slogan: "Small *poka-yoke* (defect-prevention techniques) create reliable quality for the bright future of the company."

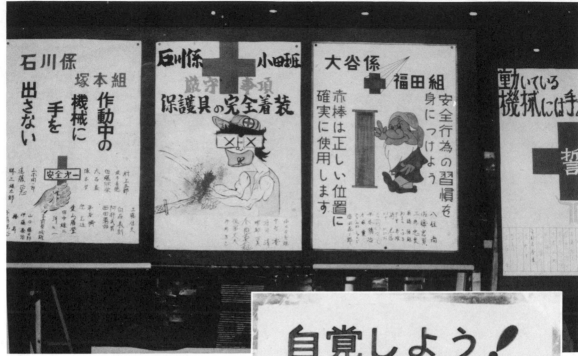

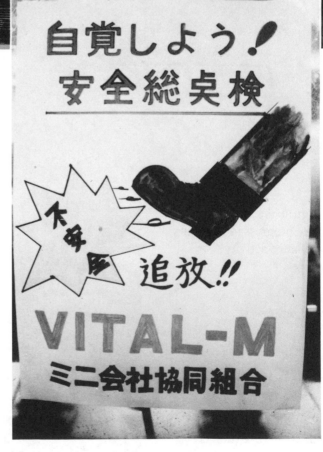

The first step of production should be safety.

Top left poster: Ishikawa subsection, Tsukamoto group
"Keep your hands out of the machine when it is on.
Safety first!"

Top middle poster: Ishikawa subsection, Fukuda group
"Wear all protective clothing."

Top right poster: Otani subsection, Fukuda group
"Make safe actions a part of your life. Keep the red pole in the right place and use it correctly."

Boot poster: "Wake up to total safety inspections.
Kick out unsafe practices."

Safety

- Production's first step should be safety.
- If we ignore safety, production becomes inefficient.
- It's important to set rules, standardize operations, and properly maintain the facilities.
- The most important thing is to build safety into the factory itself — into every process, machine, and operation — so that accidents cannot possibly occur.

In the example below, a low fence is put around a machine to prevent the operator's feet from getting caught.

Use steps to avoid accidents when descending and ascending equipment.

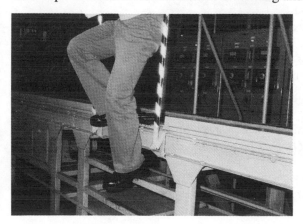

About the Editors

Hiroyuki Hirano

Hiroyuki Hirano believes just-in-time (JIT) is a theory and technique to thoroughly eliminate waste. He also calls the manufacturing process the equivalent of making music. In Japan, France, and South Korea, Mr. Hirano has led the on-site rationalization improvement movement using JIT production methods.

Some of the companies Mr. Hirano has worked with include:

Polar Synthetic Chemical Kogyo Corporation
Matsushita Denko Corporation
Sunwave Kogyo Corporation
Olympic Corporation
Ube Kyosan Corporation
Fujitsu Corporation
Yasuda Kogyo Corporation
Sharp Corporation and associated industries
Nihon Denki Corporation and associated industries
Yowazawa Densen Corporation and associated industries
Kimura Denki Manufacturing Corporation and associated industries
Fukuda ME Kogyo Corporation
Akazashina Manufacturing Corporation
Runeau Public Corporation (France)
Kumho (South Korea)
Samsung Electronics (South Korea)
Samsung Watch (South Korea)
Sani Electric (South Korea)

Selected publications and videos:

JIT Production Revolution: Supervisor's Manual, JIT Research Laboratory.
JIT Production Revolution (video, 6 tapes), Nikkan Kogyo Shinbun.
5S Comics, Nikkan Kogyo Shinbun.
Seeing Is Understanding: The Just-in-Time Production System, Nikkan Kogyo Shinbun.
Understanding Inventory Control, Nihon Jigyo Shuppan.
Poka-yoke: Improving Product Quality by Preventing Defects, H. Hirano with Nikkan Kogyo Shinbun. [This book is available in English from Productivity Press, Cambridge, MA.]
The 5S Techniques, H. Hirano et al., Nikkan Kogyo Shinbun.
Encyclopedia of Comprehensive On-Site Improvements, H. Hirano et al., Nikkan Kogyo Shinbun.
Devising and Carrying Out Poka-Yoke Zero Defects, JIT Research Laboratory.
Encyclopedia of Factory Rationalization, H. Hirano, ed., Nikkan Kogyo Shinbun.

Seeing Is Understanding: Applying the 5 Stages of MRP, H. Hirano and
O. Masashisa, Nikkan Kogyo Shinbun.
500 Selected Terms for MRP with Illustrations, H. Hirano and U. Naoki, eds.,
Nikkan Kogyo Shinbun.
MRP for Mid- and Small-Size Companies, Nikkan Kogyo Shinbun.

Dr. JT. Black

After receiving his bachelor's degree from Lehigh University, Dr. JT. Black
went to West Virginia University as an instructor in the industrial engineering
department while earning his master's degree. He then studied materials and
processes at the University of Illinois-Urbana and taught there for one year after
receiving his doctorate in mechanical and industrial engineering. He taught at the
University of Vermont, University of Rhode Island, and Ohio State University.

He is now the director of Auburn University's Advanced Manufacturing
Technology Center (AMTC) and professor of industrial engineering. The AMTC
has established a cellular manufacturing systems laboratory along with labs in
manufacturing systems modeling, robotics applications, information
resources, and metrology. Plans for other new labs are pending, including a
quality and reliability improvement lab and a lab for studying the rapid exchange
of tools and dies.

His research efforts are in two major directions: the study of integrated
manufacturing production systems (IMPSs) and the study of the machining
process. Regarding the former, he believes just-in-time manufacturing and
linked-cellular manufacturing systems are the keys to the factory with a future. He
has pioneered research in robot process capability. He has developed unique
experimental techniques to study the machining process.

Selected publications:

"Cellular Manufacturing Systems," in *Just-in-Time Manufacture* (United
Kingdom: IFS LTD., 1987).
"Machining Processes," in *Production Handbook*, 4th ed. (New York:
John Wiley & Sons, 1987).
Co-author, "Improving and Measuring Robot Process Capability," *CIM Review*,
3(4):44-49, 1987.
Co-author, "Just-in-Time, with Kanban, Manufacturing System Simulation on
Microcomputer," *Simulation*, 45(2):62-70, 1985.
Co-author, *Materials and Processes in Manufacturing*, 7th ed. (New York:
MacMillan, 1988).
"Flow Stress Model in Metal Cutting," *Transactions of ASME*, 101(4):403, 1979.
"IE's Have Roots, Too," *Industrial Engineering*, 10(5), May 1978.

Index

Adaptors, 157
Added value, 22-23
Andon (line-stop alarm lights), 174, 177
Arrangement, proper (*Seiri*), 28-29, 34,
    147, 188, 190, 199
Assembly areas, 169, 173
Assembly line, 9, 43, 53, 66, 75-77, 80
    U-shaped, 70-72, 126
Automated guided vehicles (AGVs), 24
Automated storage & retrieval system
    (AS/RSs), 24
Automobiles, 3, 25-26, 66, 68, 78, 112
Autonomation (Automation with a
    human touch), 13, 15, 134-135,
    137, 144. *See also Jidoka*
Awareness revolution, 13-15, 18, 184

Black, Dr. JT., *See* Preface, Foreword
Bodek, Norman, *See* Preface, Foreword

Casters, 16, 21, 41, 69, 87, 115, 119,
    121-122
Cells. *See* Manufacturing cells
Cellular manufacturing system. *See*
    Manufacturing cells
Cellular shop, 68
Changeover, 13, 15, 20, 43, 116, 128, 135,
    144, 146-148, 150-157
    Internal vs. external, 144, 146-147
Charts, 104-105, 108, 158, 169, 187-189
    193, 194
Cleanliness (also *Seiso*), 28-29, 63, 101
Cleanup (also *Seiketsu*), 27-29, 61,
    196-197
Computers, 193
Continuous flow, 81, 88, 93-95
Continuous improvement, P-1
Corporate culture, 18
Costs, 5, 124-125, 185
Customers, 15, 23
Cycle time, 64, 78-79, 102-105, 107-108,
    128-129

Deburring, 68, 108, 111
Decoupling, 138
Defectives. *See* Defects
Defects, 2, 5, 26, 68, 76, 78-79, 134, 141,
    159-161, 164-166, 183, 197
Diecastings, 68, 108, 126
Discipline (also *Shitsuke*), 28-29, 159,
    190, 197

Economic lot, 2
Equipment, 4, 16, 28, 32, 83, 90, 93, 119,
    123, 139, 141, 164, 177, 179-181,
    191, 193-194, 198, 203

Five S's, 14-15, 28, 30-31, 37, 39, 42-43,
    45-46, 50, 56, 58, 62-63, 68, 144,
    161, 180-181, 188, 190-191,
    195, 197
Five why's and one how (also 5W1H),
    See Why
Flexible (also Flexibility), 41, 70, 88,
    123, 144, 164, 191
Flexible manufacturing system (FMS),
    F-3, 3
Flow manufacturing, 13, 15, 17, 21, 64,
    66, 75, 80, 93-94, 138, 143, 153,
    159, 161
Improvement, 3, 5, 11, 14, 26-29, 30, 40,
    43, 58, 63, 75, 90, 99, 119, 141,
    166, 178-180, 190-191
    At a glance, 16
    Ten principles for, 19
    Surface vs. real, 24-25
    5W1H, 25
Inspection, 36, 71, 73, 75-76, 78-79, 87,
    89, 91, 107, 141, 148, 161, 163-165
    Area, 66, 133
    Devices, 33
    In-process, 77
Integrated circuit (IC) insert line, 85
Inventory control, *See* Foreword,
    Preface, 166

Jidoka. See also Autonomation, 13, 15, 110, 117, 134-135, 137, 141-143
Jigs, 32-33, 42-43, 98, 147-148, 155, 165
JIT factory revolution, 3, 5
Just-in-time (JIT), F-1, P-1, I-1, 2-3, 5, 11, 13, 15, 18, 20-21, 27, 41, 113, 166, 189, 202

Kanban, F-4, 6, 13, 15, 166-168, 170-174, 180-185, 193
  Posted (or standing), 180
  Production ordering (POKs), 168, 171
  Withdrawal (or conveyance) (WLKs), 168, 174

Layout, plant. *See also* Maps
  Assembly line, 53, 71
  Cellular, 105
  Floor, 41, 65-66, 119, 195
  Job shop, 16, 68
Leadcutting, 72, 94
Leveled production, 13, 15, 128, 131, 133, 166
Linestops, 88, 174, 177
Lot production, traditional, 2, 15-16, 20, 66-67, 76, 78, 97, 99, 152, 158

Maintenance. *See also* Safety, 13, 15, 159, 161, 198-201
Manpower reduction, 13, 15, 70, 77, 88, 117, 122, 124-126, 178
Manufacturing cells, U-shaped, 15, 17, 23, 25, 27, 64, 66-69, 72, 75-76, 79, 101-102, 104-108, 110, 113, 115-117, 122, 126-127, 144, 159, 171, 185
Manufacturing system (or Production system), 3, 11, 16, 18, 21, 24, 27, 67, 69, 71, 110, 112, 117, 124, 154, 158, 166
  Design of, *See* Foreword
  Classical, or traditional, *See* Foreword
Maps. *See also* Plant layout, 194-195
Motion, 22-23, 53, 146
Multi-process (or Multi-machine) handling, 13, 15, 17, 65, 77-78, 90, 110-113, 115, 117, 122, 126, 133, 161

Multi-skilled operators, 77, 88, 110, 122, 133, 159
Mutual line assistance, 88-90

Newly industrialized countries (NICs), *See* Introduction

Office, keeping in order, 31, 56, 58
Ohno, Taiichi. *See* Foreword
Operations, 15, 23, 27, 30, 33, 63, 65, 80, 83, 87, 102, 104-108, 122, 125, 134, 136, 146, 152-153, 158-159, 163, 168, 194, 203
Orderliness (*Seiton*), 28, 34, 43-45, 147, 188, 195
Overproduction, 22, 174

Poka-yoke (Defect-prevention), 78-79, 142, 158-159, 161
Production plan, 130
Production requirements, 70, 130, 193
Production system. *See* Manufacturing system

Quality, 11, 36, 40, 78, 102, 105, 158, 161, 166
Quality assurance (QA), 13, 15, 158

"Red tag" campaign, 32-33
Resistance encountered, 18
Rest area, 61-63, 76-77, 182

Safety. *See also* Maintenance, 13, 15, 104-105, 107-108, 159, 198-199, 202-203
Seiketsu. See Cleanup
Seiri. See Proper arrangement
Seiso. See Cleanliness
Seiton. See Orderliness
Sensor assembly, 75, 91-92, 97, 99, 134, 139, 141, 163, 165, 171, 177
Sheets, red-bordered. *See* "Red tag" campaign
Shelves, keeping in order, 6, 11, 24, 32, 36-43, 191, 194-195
Shingo, Shigeo, 79, 152
Shitsuke. See Discipline
Shot blasting, 26, 68, 93

Signboards, 174, 179-182, 184, 186, 188, 190, 193-194, 197
Single-minute exchange of die (SMED), 152
Slogans, 30, 161, 186-188, 191, 201
SMED. *See* Single-minute exchange of die
Soldering, 71-72, 94, 101
Space, 9, 28, 32, 40, 44, 58, 63, 76, 87, 117, 178
Standing (Chair-free) operations, 21, 64, 74, 76, 78-80, 85, 87-88
Stock-on-hand, 8, 102, 107-108
Storage, 4-7, 11, 24, 31, 45, 167, 170, 194
Subassemblies, 33, 66, 133, 174
Supervision, 137

TEI *See* Total employee involvement
Tool board, 48
Tools, 28, 32-33, 42-43, 48-50, 110, 137, 144, 147, 154, 176
  Hand, 48
  Cleaning, 50
  Cutting, 154-155, 174
Total employee involvement (TEI), 159
Total productive maintenance (TPM), 200-201
Toyota Motor Company, 134
Toyota Production System. *See* Foreword
Trash, 31, 35, 61

Utility closet, 50

Visual control, 13, 15, 33-34, 106, 108, 159, 161, 166, 171, 174, 187, 195

Waste, total elimination of, 16, 21-25, 27-28, 32, 40, 54, 56, 61, 71, 90, 124, 146-147, 158, 166, 176-177, 180
"Water beetles," 187
Why, asking five times, 19, 25, 151
  "5W1H Improvement," 25
Work and motion, 22-23
Work sequence, 53, 102, 105
Worktables, 56, 69, 80, 83, 85, 87, 102, 193
  Keeping in order, 53-54

Work-in-process, 9, 33, 76, 95-96
  Inventory, 30, 32, 72, 92-94, 117, 180
Worker cooperation, 88
Worker hours, reducing, 122
Workplace, 18, 28
  Design of, 179
  Keeping in order, 35, 38, 46, 48, 50

Yen appreciation, 2

Zero defects (ZD), 79, 160, 161

208

Books Available From Productivity Press

Productivity Press publishes and distributes materials on productivity, quality improvement, and employee involvement for business and industry, academia, and the general market. Many products are direct source materials from Japan that have been translated into English for the first time and are available exclusively from Productivity. Supplemental services include conferences, seminars, in-house training programs, and industrial study missions. Send for free book catalog.

Kanban and Just-In-Time at Toyota
Management Begins at the Workplace (rev.)
edited by the Japan Management Association, translated by David J. Lu

Based on seminars developed by Taiichi Ohno and others at Toyota for their major suppliers, this book is the best practical introduction to Just-In-Time available. Now in a newly expanded edition, it explains every aspect of a "pull" system in clear and simple terms — the underlying rationale, how to set up the system and get everyone involved, and how to refine it once it's in place. A groundbreaking and essential tool for companies beginning JIT implementation.
ISBN 0-915299-48-8 / 224 pages / $29.95

Introduction to TPM
Total Productive Maintenance
by Seiichi Nakajima

Total Productive Maintenance (TPM) combines the American practice of preventive maintenance with the Japanese concepts of total quality control (TQC) and total employee involvement (TEI). The result is an innovative system for equipment maintenance that optimizes effectiveness, eliminates breakdowns, and promotes autonomous operator maintenance through day-to-day activities. This book summarizes the steps involved in TPM and provides case examples from several top Japanese plants.
ISBN 0-915299-23-2 / 18 pages / $39.95

Toyota Production System
Beyond Large-Scale Production
by Taiichi Ohno

Here's the original — the first information ever published in Japan on the Toyota production system (also known as Just-In-Time manufacturing). And it was written by the man who created JIT for Toyota. In this book you will learn about the origins and development of the system, as well as its underlying philosophy. Any company aspiring to be a world class manufacturer must understand the concepts developed by Mr. Ohno. This classic is the place to start.
ISBN 0-915299-14-3 / 176 pages / $39.95

Productivity Press, Inc., Dept. BK, P.O. Box 3007, Cambridge, MA 02140 1-800-274-9911

Workplace Management

Taiichi Ohno

An in-depth view of how one of this century's leading industrial thinkers approaches problem solving and continuous improvement. Gleaned from Ohno's forty years of experimentation and innovation at Toyota Motor Co., where he created JIT, this book explains the concepts Ohno considers most important to successful management, with an emphasis on quality.
ISBN 0-915299-19-4 / 165 pages / $34.95

Just-In-Time for Today and Tomorrow

by Taiichi Ohno and Setsuo Mito

Taiichi Ohno's latest ideas are brought out in this discussion of JIT management and its application to every kind of workplace. A lively dialogue between Ohno and journalist Mito, covering topics like how easily JIT and kanban fit into this "information age," leadership imagination and decisiveness, and 7-eleven food stores.
ISBN 0-915299-20-8 / 208 pages / $34.95

A Study of the Toyota Production System
From an Industrial Engineering Viewpoint (rev.)

by Shigeo Shingo

The "green book" that started it all — the first book in English on JIT, now completely revised and re-translated. Here is Dr. Shingo's classic industrial engineering rationale for the priority of process-based over operational improvements for manufacturing. He explains the basic mechanisms of the Toyota production system in a practical and simple way so that you can apply them in your own plant.
ISBN 0-915299-17-8 / 352 pages / Price TBA (available August 1989)

Productivity Press, Inc., Dept. BK, P.O. Box 3007, Cambridge, MA 02140 1-800-274-9911

BOOKS AVAILABLE FROM PRODUCTIVITY PRESS

Christopher, William F. **Productivity Measurement Handbook**
ISBN 0-915299-05-4 / 1983 / 680 pages / looseleaf / $137.95

Ford, Henry. **Today and Tomorrow** (originally published 1926)
ISBN 0-915299-36-4 / 1988 / 302 pages / hardcover / $24.95

Fukuda, Ryuji. **Managerial Engineering: Techniques for Improving Quality and Productivity in the Workplace**
ISBN 0-915299-09-7 / 1984 / 206 pages / hardcover / $34.95

Hatakeyama, Yoshio. **Manager Revolution! A Guide to Survival in Today's Changing Workplace**
ISBN 0-915299-10-0 / 1984 / 198 pages / hardcover / $24.95

Japan Human Resources Association. **The Idea Book: Improvement Through Total Employee Involvement**
ISBN 0-915299-22-4 / 1988 / 218 pages / $49.95

Japan Management Association and Constance E. Dyer. **Canon Production System: Creative Involvement of the Total Workforce**
ISBN 0-915299-06-2 / 1987 / 251 pages / hardcover / $36.95

Japan Management Association. **Kanban and Just-In-Time at Toyota: Management Begins at the Workplace, Revised Edition,** translated by David J. Lu
ISBN 0-915299-08-9 / 1986 / 224 pages / hardcover / $29.95

Karatsu, Hajime. **Tough Words for American Industry**
ISBN 0-915299-25-9 / 1988 / 179 pages / hardcover / $24.95

Karatsu, Hajime. **TQC Wisdom of Japan: Managing for Total Quality Control**
ISBN 0-915299-18-6 / 1988 / 138 pages / hardcover / $29.95

Lu, David J. **Inside Corporate Japan: The Art of Fumble-Free Management**
ISBN 0-915299-16-X / 1987 / 278 pages / hardcover / $24.95

Mizuno, Shigeru (ed.) **Management for Quality Improvement: The 7 New QC Tools**
ISBN 0-915299-29-1 / 1988 / 326 pages / hardcover / $59.95

Nakajima, Seiichi. **Introduction to Total Productive Maintenance**
ISBN 0-915299-23-2 / 1988 / 129 pages / $39.95

Nikkan Kogyo Shimbun. **Poka-yoke: Improving Product Quality by Preventing Defects**
ISBN 0-915299-31-3 / 1988 / 288 pages / $49.95

Ohno, Taiichi. **Toyota Production System: Beyond Large-Scale Production**
ISBN 0-915299-14-3 / 1988 / 176 pages / hardcover / $39.95

Ohno, Taiichi. **Workplace Management**
ISBN 0-915299-19-4 / 1988 / 176 pages / hardcover / $34.95

Ohno, Taiichi and Setsuo Mito. **Just-In-Time for Today and Tomorrow: A Total Management System**
ISBN 0-915299-20-8 / 1988 / 176 pages / hardcover / $34.95

Productivity Press, Inc., Dept. BK, P.O. Box 3007, Cambridge, MA 02140 1-800-274-9911

Shingo, Shigeo. **Non-Stock Production: The Shingo System for Continuous Improvement**
ISBN 0-915299-30-5 / 1988 / 480 pages / hardcover / $75.00

Shingo, Shigeo. **A Revolution in Manufacturing: The SMED System,** translated by Andrew P. Dillon
ISBN 0-915299-03-8 / 1985 / 383 pages / hardcover / $65.00

Shingo, Shigeo. **Zero Quality Control: Source Inspection and the Poka-yoke System,** translated by Andrew P. Dillon
ISBN 0-915299-07-0 / 1986 / 328 pages / hardcover / $65.00

Shingo, Shigeo. **The Sayings of Shigeo Shingo: Key Strategies for Plant Improvement,** translated by Andrew P. Dillon
ISBN 0-915299-15-1 / 1987 / 207 pages / hardcover / $36.95

Shinohara, Isao (ed.) **New Production System: JIT Crossing Industry Boundaries**
ISBN 0-915299-21-6 / 1988 / 218 pages / hardcover / $34.95

AUDIO-VISUAL PROGRAMS

Shingo, Shigeo. **The SMED System,** translated by Andrew P. Dillon
ISBN 0-915299-11-9 / 181 slides / 40 minutes / $749.00
ISBN 0-915299-27-5 / 2 videos / 40 minutes / $749.00

Shingo, Shigeo, **The Poka-yoke System**, translated by Andrew P. Dillon
ISBN 0-915299-13-5 / 224 slides / 45 minutes / $749.00
ISBN 0-915299-28-3 / 2 videos / 45 minutes / $749.00

TO ORDER: Write, phone or fax Productivity Press, Dept. BK, P.O. Box 3007, Cambridge, MA 02140, phone 1-800-274-9911, fax 617-868-3524.
Send check or charge to your credit card (American Express, Visa, MasterCard accepted).

U.S. ORDERS: Add $3 shipping for first book, $1 each additional. CT residents add 7.5% and MA residents 5% sales tax.

FOREIGN ORDERS: Payment must be made in U.S. dollars. For Canadian orders, add $8 shipping for first book, $1 each additional. Orders to other countries are on a pro forma basis; please indicate shipping method desired.

NOTE: Prices subject to change without notice.

Productivity Press, Inc., Dept. BK, P.O. Box 3007, Cambridge, MA 02140 1-800-274-9911

UTAH STATE UNIVERSITY PARTNERS PROGRAM

Shigeo Shingo Medallion

Shigeo Shingo Prize for Manufacturing Excellence

announces the

Shigeo Shingo Prizes for Manufacturing Excellence

Awarded for Manufacturing Excellence Based on the Work of Shigeo Shingo

for North American Businesses, Students and Faculty

ELIGIBILITY

Businesses: Applications are due in late January. They should detail the quality and productivity improvements achieved through Shingo's manufacturing methods and similar techniques. Letters of intent are required by mid-November of the previous year.

Students: Applicants from accredited schools must apply by letter before November 15, indicating what research is planned. Papers must be received by early March.

Faculty: Applicants from accredited schools must apply by letter before November 15, indicating the scope of papers planned, and submit papers by the following March.

CRITERIA

Businesses: Quality and productivity improvements achieved by using Shingo's Scientific Thinking Mechanism (STM) and his methods, such as Single-Minute-Exchange of Die (SMED), Poka-yoke (defect prevention), Just-In-Time (JIT), and Non-Stock Production (NSP), or similar techniques.

Students: Creative research on quality and productivity improvements through the use and extension of Shingo's STM and his manufacturing methods: SMED, NSP, and Poka-yoke.

Faculty: Papers publishable in professional journals based on empirical, conceptual or theoretical applications and extensions of Shingo's manufacturing methods for quality and productivity improvements: SMED, Poka-yoke, JIT, and NSP.

PRIZES

Awards will be presented by Shigeo Shingo at Utah State University's annual Partners Productivity Seminar, held in April in Logan, Utah.

Five graduate and five undergraduate student awards of $2,000, $1,500, and $1,000 to first, second, and third place winners, respectively, and $500 to fourth and fifth place winners.

Three faculty awards of $3,000, $2,000 and $1,000, respectively.

Six Shigeo Shingo Medallions to the top three large and small business winners.

SHINGO PRIZE COMMITTEE

Committee members representing prestigious business, professional, academic and governmental organizations worldwide will evaluate the applications and select winners, assisted by a technical examining board.

Application forms and contest information may be obtained from the Shingo Prize Committee, College of Business, UMC 3521, Utah State University, Logan, UT, 84322, 801-750-2281. All English language books by Dr. Shingo can be purchased from the publisher, Productivity Press, P.O. Box 3007, Cambridge, MA 02140: call 1-800-274-9911 or 617-497-5146.

Japan's "Dean of Quality Consultants"

Dr. Shigeo Shingo is, quite simply, the world's leading expert on improving the manufacturing process. Known as "Dr. Improvement" in Japan, he is the originator of the Single-Minute Exchange of Die (SMED) concept and the Poka-yoke defect prevention system and one of the developers of the Just-In-Time production system that helped make Toyota the most productive automobile manufacturer in the world. His work now helps hundreds of other companies worldwide save billions of dollars in manufacturing costs annually.

The most sought-after consultant in Japan, Dr. Shingo has trained more than 10,000 people in 100 companies. He established and is President of Japan's highly-regarded Institute of Management Improvement and is the author of numerous books, including *Revolution in Manufacturing: The SMED System* and *Zero Quality Control: Source Inspection and the Poka-yoke System*. His newest book, *Non-Stock Production*, concentrates on expanding U.S. manufacturers' understanding of stockless production.

Dr. Shingo's genius is his understanding of exactly why products are manufactured the way they are, and then transforming that understanding into a workable system for low-cost, high-quality production. In the history of international manufacturing, Shingo stands alongside such pioneers as Robert Fulton, Henry Ford, Frederick Taylor, and Douglas McGregor as one of the key figures in the quest for improvement.

His world-famous SMED system is known as "The Heart of Just-In-Time Manufacturing" for (1) reducing set-up time from hours to minutes; (2) cutting lead time from months to days; (3) slashing work-in-progress inventory by up to 90%; (4) involving employees in team problem solving; (5) 99% improvement in quality; and (6) 70% reduction in floor space.

> *Shigeo Shingo has been called the father of the second great revolution in manufacturing.*
>
> — Quality Control Digest

The money-saving, profit-making ideas... set forth by Shingo could do much to help U.S. manufacturers reduce set-up time, improve quality and boost productivity ... all for very little cash.

Tooling & Production Magazine

When Americans think about quality today, they often think of Japan. But when the Japanese think of quality, they are likely to think of Shigeo Shingo, ... architect of Toyota's now famous production system.

Boardroom Report

Shingo's visit to our plant was significant in making breakthroughs in productivity we previously thought impossible. The benefits... are more far-reaching than I ever anticipated.

Gifford M. Brown, Plant Mgr.
Ford Motor Company